W9-CIB-746

GUERRILLA WARFARE

Casemate Short History

GUERRILLA
WARFARE

KINGS OF REVOLUTION

Peter Polack

CASEMATE
Oxford & Philadelphia

Published in Great Britain and
the United States of America in 2018 by
CASEMATE PUBLISHERS
The Old Music Hall, 106–108 Cowley Road, Oxford OX4 1JE, UK
1950 Lawrence Road, Havertown, PA 19083, USA

© Peter Polack 2018

Paperback Edition: ISBN 978-1-61200-675-8
Digital Edition: ISBN 978-1-61200-676-5 (epub)

All rights reserved. No part of this book may be reproduced or transmitted in
any form or by any means, electronic or mechanical including photocopying,
recording or by any information storage and retrieval system, without
permission from the publisher in writing.

A CIP record for this book is available from the British Library

Printed in Czech Republic by FINIDR, s.r.o.

Typeset in India by Versatile PreMedia Services. www.versatilepremedia.com

For a complete list of Casemate titles, please contact:

CASEMATE PUBLISHERS (UK)
Telephone (01865) 241249
Email: casemate-uk@casematepublishers.co.uk
www.casematepublishers.co.uk

CASEMATE PUBLISHERS (US)
Telephone (610) 853-9131
Fax (610) 853-9146
Email: casemate@casematepublishers.com
www.casematepublishers.com

A minha filha fiel Olivia a guerrilha de Sun Tzu corporativa moderna desejando lhe horizontes sem fim da independência com o grande amor de um pai devotado e orgulhoso.

Papa

Do not stand at my grave and weep,
I am not there, I do not sleep.
I am a thousand winds that blow.
I am the diamond glints on snow.
I am the sun on ripened grain.
I am the gentle autumn rain.
When you awaken in the morning hush,
I am the swift, uplifting rush
Of quiet birds in circling flight.
I am the soft star-shine at night.
Do not stand at my grave and cry.
I am not there, I did not die.

Mary Frye (1932)

To the many millions who followed the few to liberation or condemnation this work seeks neither approval nor rejection.

Whenever there is conflict in distribution of resources or suppression of human rights or targeting of any group, this book will be a useful guide for governments of oppression, great and small. Perhaps it would be better as a window of prescience before the mayhem inevitably ensues.
Often times the seed of guerrilla is planted as simply in a street fruit vendor pressed to the point of self-immolation.

Not only will governments fall but regions turn to turmoil over the temporary peace of inequality.
They harvest a crop not of juicy fruit but merely the horrors of death and destruction.

CONTENTS

'Let every soul be subject unto the higher powers. For there is no power but of God: the powers that be are ordained of God. Whosoever therefore resisteth the power, resisteth the ordinance of God: and they that resist shall receive to themselves damnation. For rulers are not a terror to good works, but to the evil. Wilt thou then not be afraid of the power? do that which is good, and thou shalt have praise of the same: For he is the Minister of God to thee for good. But if you do that which is evil, be afraid; for he beareth not the sword in vain: for he is the minister of God, a revenger to execute wrath upon him that doeth evil.'

Romans 13: 1–4, The Bible (King James Version)

'The guerrilla must move amongst the people as a fish swims in the sea.'

Mao Zedong, 1946

'The chief says burn everything. By everything he means everything. Women, children everything.'

General Ben Ben, Luanda, Angola, 1992

'Success has many fathers, but failure is an orphan.'

Attributed to Publius Cornelius Tacitus, *Agricola*, AD 98

INTRODUCTION

The concept of guerrilla warfare is not decades, but many centuries old, with the earliest writing on the subject by Sun Tzu dating back to the 6th century BC. Some guerrilla tactics are probably as old as the first armed groups of cavemen, being a natural evolution of conflict between groups of disproportionate sizes. One of the earliest examples of guerrilla tactics deployed by a consummate institutional military leader was Roman general Fabius Maximus's evade and harassment actions undertaken against Hannibal's columns in the 2nd century BC, much to the dismay of the Roman senate who had argued for a classic offensive battle.

This book is a compendium of some prominent worldwide guerrilla leaders beginning with William Wallace in the 13th century to modern-day Sri Lanka, profiling each leader to analyse their career, military tactics and political strategy. The leaders included are all homegrown in extended guerrilla campaigns, many of whom ended up as the first leaders of their countries or liberators of entire regions such as Simon Bolivar. It includes victories and defeats in an effort to tease out not only effective guerrilla tactics but counter-insurgency strategies with some likelihood of success. Whilst there is certain to be punditry as to the exclusion of some lesser guerrilla fighters and leaders, the selection in this book is for the most part limited to 'successful' guerrilla leaders or those who were successful in changing their society. In this case, success can also mean an enduring symbol of encouragement for self-determination. Che Guevara, though popular, was not included. He was a commander of two minor, failed campaigns in the Congo and Bolivia, the last

Guerrillas certainly existed in **ancient Greece and Rome** as these empires sought to grow and often enslave enemies in the quest for expansion. Roman history is replete of the many states that resisted the great republic's domination, premier among them was the most successful enemy of Rome, Hannibal of Carthage. One of the earliest examples of enslavement was of the Jews by the Roman Empire that led to many uprisings including one that ended at Masada with the mass suicide of rebel Jewish fighters.

Masada fortress Israel 2007. (Andrew Shiva/Wikimedia Commons)

of which led to his death. That scenario played out against a local population of scarce resources and inhospitable areas of operation. It would be a very steep hill to emulate and exceed Bolivar in Latin America.

This selection provides a wide cross-section over time, region and country, but has had to exclude many other individuals: Canadian Louis Riel, Haitian Toussaint L'Overture, Cuban Antonio Maceo,

Modern guerrilla warfare or insurgency has given rise lately to the term **asymmetrical warfare**, in essence the conflict between two opposing forces of different strength and strategy. This differs from the classic historical conflict and war where opposing forces were well matched in size and weaponry. The concept of guerrilla warfare encompassing rural areas of remote operation that offer vast areas of camouflage from the enemy has become muted as conflicts have become increasingly based on population centres that more resemble the siege of Stalingrad than the jungles of Colombia. The advice expounded by Mao Zedong that: 'the guerrilla must move amongst the people as a fish swims in the sea' with his experiences of long marches over remote countryside regions of China has now has to be applied to a more urbanised context. The term 'insurgent', 'freedom fighter' or even 'jihadi' is fast replacing guerrilla.

Farabundo Marti of El Salvador, Nicaraguan Augusto Cesar Sandino, Irish Michael Collins, Ethiopian Haile Selassie, Israeli Menachem Begin, Mozambican Samora Machel, Peruvian Shining Path Chairman Gonzalo, Mexican Zapatista Sub-Commandante Marcos, and Chechen Shamil Basayev.

This is not meant to be an all-encompassing historical record of every detail of every battle fought by the guerrilla leaders, but a synopsis where appropriate to illustrate common guerrilla concepts that have existed and been utilised for centuries, with reliable success.

There is no romanticism in being a guerrilla or insurgent. As Eden Pastora, Commandante Cero famously said: 'The first thing we revolutionaries lose is our wives. The last thing we lose is our lives. In between our women and our lives, we lose our freedom, our happiness, our means of living.' In 1991, I met him very early one morning in Guanacaste, Costa Rica transporting fish in a small pick-up to sustain himself and his family. On 22 August 1978 Commandante Cero led a group disguised as Nicaraguan National Guard soldiers to seize the National Palace, many Congress Deputies as well as close associates and family

Commandante Cero and the author, Guanacaste, Costa Rica, December 1991. (Miguel Ortega)

of the now deceased dictator, Somoza. After payment of ransom money as well as release of many political prisoners, including top politicians of Nicaragua today, the hostages were released amidst much propaganda.

Eden Pastora Gomez was born in 1937 and co-founded the Sandino Revolutionary Front in 1959, becoming a guerrilla in the Pancasan campaign of 1967 which began in the town of Pancasan located in central Nicaragua. After leading the capture of the Nicaraguan Assembly, he became commander of the Southern Front and then Vice-Minister of Defence upon the Sandinistas taking power until 1980. Disputes with the Sandinista leadership led him to start operations against them during the Contra War before exiling himself to Costa Rica where he obtained citizenship in the 1990s. He returned to Nicaragua in 2010 after settling differences with the Sandinista government who put him in charge of dredging the Rio San Juan as part of the proposed Nicaragua canal project with the Chinese.

Commandante Cero (Eden Pastora), Nicaragua Costa Rica border, c. 1980. (The Tico Times)

It would be helpful for future world security that citizens of countries that have active local **militia groups**, both government and private who associate lawfully, appreciate that these same units may often be the last defence of the defenceless in the all too common scenario of conflict and invasion. The only certain thing is that history will repeat itself. These can often be as simple as a parochial gun club if properly regulated being restricted to the fit, the brave and the competent.

The term **guerrilla** comes from the Spanish word for war, *guerra* which itself has origins in the old German word for quarrel, *werra*. It first arose in the 19th century to describe Spanish irregulars in the Peninsula War, part of the Napoleonic Wars and was probably used by supporting British troops, to characterise Spanish militia fighting throughout the countryside in a non-traditional, ad hoc manner which tied down the invading French army who were employing traditional military tactics.

It is of interest that the common usage of the world guerrilla was born in a conflict between two countries that had very similar words for war – *guerre* in French and *guerra* in Spain – however the Spanish term oft used is *la guerra*, the feminine form similar to *la lucha*, the struggle. It is somewhat contradictory that the feminine form of a word is used to describe something a woman would not usually support as mother, wife or political leader, war. There are of course some exceptions such as Celtic queen Boadicea, and Mariana Grajales Coello, mother of Cuban independence fighter Antonio Maceo. The term guerrilla has evolved over the years to mean insurgents or freedom fighters regardless of gender but in strict usage from the Spanish origin a male fighter would be a *guerrillero* and a female *guerrillera*.

There are many common elements to the rise of guerrilla warfare across the world and across history. Namely, oppression of a particular group, wide economic disparity between working and ownership classes, racial or religious division and imperialist ambitions. Historically, expansive gaps in wealth often combine with deprivation of rights and opportunity or even outright subjugation to light the fire of resistance. These were prevalent features in the American Revolution which liberated almost an entire continent, the independence wars in Africa and most recently the struggle to preserve regimes in the Middle East amidst theological strife. Disappointingly, the result of the latter two, has only led to more abuse of power. A more modern example of guerrilla wars emanating from racial division was the extensive multi-country armed rebellion due to the system of apartheid in South Africa that spilled over into Namibia and Angola.

The most recent scenario of a successful but protracted guerrilla campaign is the FARC of Colombia who recently entered into peace accords with the Government of Colombia. This is the natural end to a guerrilla-based conflict when they lay down their arms having achieved some or all of their reasonable objectives before re-entering the fabric of society outside a war zone. The phrase that common sense is not common should not be applied to an entire country but for their pragmatic President Juan Manuel Santos, who defied all odds and even some of his core supporters, to force through peace proving someone had the requisite common sense. Colombia can now bloom like their famous roses.

There have been many instances of a conceptual natural end that defies realisation as rebel groups repeatedly enter and depart a peace process such as the Renamo of Mozambique. A useful reminder for those guerrilla leaders is the hunt and killing of Jonas Savimbi in 2002 in his home turf of Moxico, Angola after repeatedly delaying peace in the elusive quest for ultimate power.

Whilst this effort has embraced many competent guerrilla leaders of great repute, at the conclusion of this undertaking, the guerrilla 'king' who stood out most was probably the least known, General Koos de la Rey. Others will come to their own conclusion, but in terms of a tactician who, like many men of war, still retained some humanity, he sought only to embrace peace for what he considered his country, and was willing to lay down arms when necessary. In the fullness, Koos de la Rey was unmatched.

Readers are commended to watch the outstanding documentary on guerrilla life during the FMLN guerrilla struggle in El Salvador narrated by Martin Sheen appropriately entitled *In the Name of the People*. The main guerrilla leader in the film, Commandante Ramon, who did not survive the struggle, displayed the many essential characteristics of a successful guerrilla leader: cadre discipline, over-arching strategy, competent tactics on the run, and compassion. A guerrilla leader must of necessity be relentless and ruthless in pursuit of the aims of the struggle and no better example is that of the FARC leader Manuel Marulanda. From a mere youth, he rose to leadership of the FARC and was able to persist until his death from natural causes in 2008 when the FARC were at the height of their power. Shortly thereafter the Colombian government began a strategy of targeted killings of FARC leaders and psychological warfare which eventually forced the FARC to the peace table. The FARC also suffered a major blow in 2008 when several hostages, including former presidential candidate Ingrid Betancourt as well as three Americans, were handed over by a FARC commander who was also captured after an extensive subterfuge campaign. This was followed up in 2010 with the Colombian Army Christmas campaign when several tall trees in well-known guerrilla areas were lit up with a sign telling guerrillas they could come home. This strategy led to several hundred defections. In a similar action, in Christmas 2013, the Colombian government sent seven thousand small LED-lit plastic balls containing defection encouragement messages down rivers frequented by guerrillas.

Specific leadership assassinations are not a new concept in anti-guerrilla warfare but in recent years such strategies have been successful against targeted assassinations of Hamas leaders in Palestine, against the FARC by Colombia, the Taliban by the USA and ISIS commanders by Coalition forces. In the case of the two latter groups, this has not resulted in progress towards peace talks but a succession of new leaders. The strategy has its limitations. As in all things guerrilla, there comes a time to seek peace.

A reliable key to the battlefield success of the guerrilla can be drawn not from some commander's brilliant but isolated idea, an officers' conference or prior battle research but merely the regularity with which that recipe for victory, has been repeated throughout the centuries. For example the tactic of exploiting a choke point has been observed from Stirling Bridge in Scotland to the bombing of the key ball-bearing factories of Schweinfurt in Germany during World War II. The concentration of opposing forces whether in populated Mosul or the isolated Jaffna peninsula of Sri Lanka means that a siege, retreat or ambush will become an inescapable kill box for the scouts, column or army.

Finally, the lessons of guerrilla warfare can still be encapsulated in the Sun Tzu's centuries-old recommendation to avoid the strong and attack the weak. It is a lesson useful beyond guerrilla warfare, equally applicable to personal life, career and business, unlikely a comparison as this may seem. However, grand and petty dictators

A **guerrilla movement** usually follows a narrow political agenda whereas a **guerrilla revolution** will of necessity combine national groups of differing political persuasions to seek regime change. As is the case of Libya, this can also mean a split in the post-revolution period amongst the self -same groups that together brought change.

are forewarned that the road to hubris could end in an isolated desert culvert, devoid of friendly forces, leading to summary execution, as the one-time revolutionary Muammar Gaddafi found out.

TIMELINE

1297   Battle of Stirling Bridge, Scotland where William Wallace defeated the English invaders

1298   Battle of Falkirk, Scotland where William Wallace was defeated by the English invaders

1305   Execution of William Wallace in London after capture by the English

1776   The United States Declaration of Independence; the battle of Long Island which George Washington lost and Trenton which George Washington won

1777   Battle of Princeton: a second victory for George Washington

1781   British General Cornwallis surrenders to George Washington after the battle of Yorktown

1810   Declaration of independence by Venezuelan leaders

1813   Battle of Cucuta in Colombia, Decree of War to the Death by Simon Bolivar against Spanish

1817   The execution of General Manuel Piar on order of Simon Bolivar

1818   Publication of *Correo del Orinoco* by Simon Bolivar

1819   Battles of Vargas Swamp and Boyaca won by Simon Bolivar's forces

1820   Spanish armistice after defeat by Simon Bolivar

1830   Death of Simon Bolivar

1880   First Anglo-Boer War in South Africa between Boers and British

1899   Second Anglo-Boer War; battles of Modder River and Magersfontein won by Boers

1901   Battle of Masmak Fort, Riyadh, Kingdom of Saudi Arabia won by King Ibn Saud

1902	Battles of Ysterspruit and Tweebosch in the Boer War won by Boers
	Battle of Dilam, Kingdom of Saudi Arabia won by King Ibn Saud
1911	Xinhai Revolution in China
1914	Death of South African General Jacobus 'Koos' de la Rey en route to Potchefstroom military camp
1915	Treaty of Darin between Britain and the Kingdom of Saudi Arabia
1921	Battle of Ha'il, Kingdom of Saudi Arabia Establishment of the Communist Party in China
1922	Treaty of Uqair between Britain and the Kingdom of Saudi Arabia
1929	Battle of Sibilla, Kingdom of Saudi Arabia won by King Ibn Saud
1930	Battle of Jiangxi, China won by Mao Zedong
	Imprisonment of General Vo Nguyen Giap at Lao Bao prison, Quang Tri province, Vietnam
1932	Declaration of the Kingdom of Saudi Arabia by King Abdul Aziz Bin Abdul Rahman Al Saud
1934	The Long March, China by Mao Zedong
1941	Vo Nguyen Giap appointed military leader of the Viet Minh
1945	2 September: Ho Chi Minh declares the independence of the Democratic Republic of Vietnam
1949	Proclamation of the People's Republic of China by Mao Zedong
1954	Defeat of French by Vietnamese forces at battle of Dien Bien Phu, Vietnam
	Destruction of retreating French GM 100 unit at Mang Yang Pass

1959	Eden Pastora Gomez, Commandante Cero, co-founded the Sandino Revolutionary Front known as the Sandinistas in Nicaragua
1965	Battle of the Ia Drang Valley, Vietnam between US and Vietnamese forces
1966	Creation of Revolutionary Armed Forces of Colombia (FARC)
	Creation of the Uniao Nacional para a Independencia Total de Angola or The National Union for the Total Independence of Angola (UNITA)
1968	Battle of Khe Sanh, Vietnam between US and Vietnamese forces
1972	Sri Lanka leaves the Commonwealth and becomes a republic
1973	Paris Peace Accords between USA and Vietnam
1975	Angola granted independence by Portugal
1976	Creation of Liberation Tigers of Tamil Eelam or LTTE by Velupillai Prabhakaran in Sri Lanka
1977	FARC temporary seizure of the town of La Macarena, Meta region, Columbia
1978	Commandante Cero seizes the National Palace in Managua, Nicaragua
1986	LTTE destroy Air Lanka flight 512 at the Bandaranaike International Airport, Sri Lanka
1987	Battle of Cuito Cuanavale, Angola Operation *Vadamarachchi* or *Liberation* against LTTE in Sri Lanka
1990	LTTE siege attack on Kokavil Sri Lankan Army base
1991	Indian Prime Minister Rajiv Gandhi killed by female LTTE suicide bomber in Sri Lanka Battle of Elephant Pass between LTTE and Sri Lankan Army

1992	Angola election
1993	President Premadasa of Sri Lanka killed by LTTE bicycle-borne IED
1994	LTTE commander Gopalaswamy Mahendraraja executed in Sri Lanka
1995	Start of battles of Eelam in Sri Lanka
1996	LTTE Destruction of Sri Lankan army base at Mullativu, Sri Lanka
1998	FARC given demilitarised zone in southern Colombia
2001	LTTE attack Bandaranaike International Airport and Katunayake military airbase, Sri Lanka
2002	UNITA leader Jonas Savimbi killed in Moxico, Angola
	Election of Colombian President Alvaro Uribe
2005	General Sarath Fonseka appointed chief of Sri Lankan Army
2007	LTTE Air Force and Black Tiger suicide soldiers attack Anuradhapura Air Force Base, Sri Lanka
2008	Death of Manuel Marulanda in Colombia Operation *Jaque*, rescue of FARC hostages by Colombian Army
2009	LTTE leader Velupillai Prabhakaran killed in Sri Lanka
2013	Death of General Vo Nguyen Giap in Vietnam
2016	Colombian government and FARC agree peace treaty

CHAPTER 1

WILLIAM WALLACE, SCOTLAND

What was most extraordinary about the guerrilla leader William Wallace was the speed with which a virtual unknown rose up to national leadership and the short time between his first action, the killing of the English sheriff of Lanark in May 1297 and his victory at the battle of Stirling Bridge on 11 September 1297, a mere four months later. Even more compelling was that within a year he had vacated his position as Guardian of Scotland in favour of Robert the Bruce, the future king of Scotland, before disappearing until capture and vile execution on the orders of King Edward I of England in 1305 – in total only eight years between rise and demise.

Given the extent of time that has passed and the difficulties of early record keeping it is unsurprising that so little is known about the early life of Wallace. Much reliance has been placed by some on the extensive but criticised poem about William Wallace by Scottish poet Blind Harry entitled *The Wallace* composed in the late 15th century. Bridging the gap between fact and fiction, commonly supported by the Lubeck letter believed to have been sent on his behalf, Wallace came from a recognised family of tenant farmers in Elderslie, Renfrewshire or Ayrshire in central Scotland and is thought to be the son of Alan Wallace. Whatever the historical views, what is clear was that this was a singular man who became not only a Scottish icon but a symbol for freedom fighters worldwide. Perhaps Reverend J. S. Watson said it best:

If there has been any exaggeration of his merits, in narratives oral or written, in subsequent days, it must still be believed that he would never have become such an object of panegyric among his contemporaries, unless he had signally transcended other men.

Sometimes it is often best to seek a compromise of more proximate records of history, however limited, with those that revisit research in the modern era.

The conflict that gave rise to the emergence of William Wallace was a dispute over the throne of Scotland between Baliol and Robert the Bruce that led, after some manoeuvring by King Edward I of England, to war and the submission of Baliol, who had aligned himself with the French. In the end, King Edward, known as Longshanks due to his height, carried away the Scottish throne of stone from Scone and destroyed records pointing to Scottish independence or the inferiority of the English. After Baliol spent a period in the Tower of London he was exiled to France where he died.

Very often a guerrilla leader will arise in circumstances of political turmoil such as conflict on the succession to a throne, the opposing forces of a civil war on the cusp of independence – such as in China in 1949, Angola in 1975 and the ethnic Balkanisation of Sri Lanka in 1976.

Edward then appointed a governor-general of Scotland and filled as many posts as possible with English immigrants, a template adopted by England throughout the ages, and even to this day in their few tiny remaining far-flung possessions. The original governor-general soon vacated the post leaving the ruthless Chief Justice Ormesby with Lord-Treasurer Cressingham to oppress and loot Scotland, a historical mandate repeated throughout English possessions for centuries. Edward then ordered a further requirement that the landed gentry of Scotland swear allegiance to him under penalty of imprisonment or become a fugitive, which added to a growing resentment and hatred of the English occupiers. Here one of the primary elements of successful guerrilla warfare presents itself – when indigenous people have their land occupied by a foreign or local group that proceeds to regulate and often exploit a newly created and previously peaceful underclass.

One of the Scottish lairds removed from power during this period was the Earl of Angus, who had presided over the town of Dundee. Dundee became occupied by an English freebooter from Cumberland called Selby whose presence at that convenient location allowed more of his ilk to use it as a stopping point into the interior of Scotland. It was a period of lawlessness, oppression and violence by a series of mini potentates throughout Scotland as untitled and landless Englishmen seized on the opportunity to take land and make wealth. At the time Wallace was living in Dundee with his uncle and after a dispute between local and English officials including Selby's son over a game of quoits, Wallace killed the son with his sword. One account has Wallace fleeing Dundee after the incident in woman's dress. This same record has Wallace being from Ellerslie in Renfrewshire and the son of Sir Malcolm Wallace but later research, including the Lubeck letter, has cast great doubt on this rendition.

The guerrilla leader often begins from nondescript and forgettable beginnings and from one single incident begins their climb to ultimate leadership. For George Washington it was Trenton, for Mao the Long March and King Ibn Saud, the capture of Masmak Fort in Riyadh.

A common facet of guerrilla leaders before establishing a safe haven is to evade capture by different disguises and multiple locations or safe houses. What seems certain is that Wallace, while a relatively young man, left the vicinity of his immediate problem and began to journey across Scotland to forestall capture often in the company of family or using family connections for safe haven. A common tale is that a dispute with the William Hazelrig, sheriff of Lanark, over Wallace's new bride resulted in her death leading to a reprisal by Wallace to attack and kill the sheriff along with several others. A. F. Murison in his 1898 book, originally published as *Sir William Wallace*, describes a series of events under the title 'Guerrilla Warfare', and quotes William Shakespeare's *Henry IV*: 'Now, for our consciences, the arms are fair, when the intent of bearing them is just'.

Other tales told of Wallace include the killing of several men associated with English nobleman Sir Edward de Percy over an attempt to seize fish from Wallace. There was the death of an Englishman at Ayr following a bet about whether he could sustain a blow from Wallace – he could not; the killing of a servant of Sir Reginald Crawford, the sheriff of Ayr, in a dispute over fish in the market whereupon Wallace was incarcerated, disposed of as dead, before mysteriously recovering; and the killing of an English squire and his followers with a rusty sword. Many of these were drawn from the Blind Harry poem.

While accounts vary on the period after the incidents at Dundee and Lanark, most agree that the young Wallace became a fugitive and nominal parochial leader for the like-minded who opposed the English occupation of their towns and lands. Moving frequently with a growing band of followers, he began a series of attacks not only to support his group but to inflict destruction on his enemies, which began to raise his profile. Several incidents ascribed to him involve great acts of violence and killings not in perpetuation of some nationalist sentiment but resolution of domestic and social disputes, which happened to leave English corpses with some important connections.

All accounts tend to culminate with his participation at the battle of Stirling Bridge in 1297. This battle was preceded by what is often referred to as the rising in Lanark after the killing of the sheriff. At this time Wallace was a fugitive from the authorities, which could be compared with the situation of former political fugitive, and later Vietnamese general, Vo Nguyen Giap in 1930. They were both strong nationalists that ended up in wars of independence, with Giap eventually enjoying the greater success.

Shortly after Lanark, anti-English forces within Scotland, attracted by the small but bold actions of Wallace and some of them with petty axes of their own to grind, joined up with his forces. They proceeded to roam central Scotland in sufficient numbers to win all encounters. At the time, the English had retreated from all of Scotland north of the Forth River except for Dundee and Stirling, which subsequently drew the attention of Wallace and his followers. They marched on Dundee and laid siege in August 1297. The Scottish forces – as was common at the time and is still seen today, for example in present-day Syria – was an alliance of forces, some with different agendas. The joint force was under the leadership of Wallace and Andrew Moray or Murray which was confirmed by the Lubeck letter sent in both their names as leaders of Scotland. The Forth was a barrier to the north-east and Stirling was a critical geographical junction for any English army wishing to march on Scotland.

A guerrilla leader draws on small initial successes to gather confidence and spread his fame across the country, which is a double-edged sword. The benefit of attracting material support and fighters is tempered with increased attention from the prevailing authorities, which will limit general anonymity or travelling to further the cause. As the size of the resistance group increases so does the number of the hierarchy, which impairs command and control by single decision making to avoid conflict and confusion among lower commanders.

During this period, Edward Longshanks departed for a brief military venture in Flanders, charging his reluctant governor of Scotland, John de Warenne, who was then in northern England, to move a part of the army of England north to repel Scottish rebels and re-establish English authority. In the summer of 1297, after a series of small successes, William Wallace prepared to fight the battle that would become the centre tenet of his reputation as a guerrilla leader, against a large English force led by John de Warenne, the Earl of Surrey, with Sir Hugh de Cressingham, the English-appointed and much-hated treasurer for Scotland. Originally intending to encircle Dundee, Wallace changed course on hearing of the approach of the English force that was determined to bring their authority to bear over all of Scotland.

Wallace halted at the small abbey of Cambuskenneth in a village close to Stirling Castle, surrounded on three sides by the River Forth across which the English encamped preparing for battle.

For a man uneducated in formal military strategy, Wallace had picked an optimal position which was surrounded and protected by a flowing river, high banks to limit cavalry and high ground to watch any approach. As it was summer, the hours of daylight were long which enabled his forces to keep a close watch on its enemies, who were preparing to fight within eyesight. The benefit of local

Cambuskenneth Abbey. (Jo Woolf)

knowledge, and an intrinsic understanding of geography, obstacles and opportunities form a core skill for any guerrilla leader with any aspiration of success.

As was common at that time, there was a certain amount of pre-battle parley through intermediaries, in this case two Dominican friars from the nearby abbey. This type of communication has seen a resurgence in recent Middle Eastern conflicts where warring parties are often from the same country, religion and general tribal area.

Warenne was probably emboldened by the numerical inferiority of the Scottish rebels on the field of battle and the ease of the swearing of loyalty to King Edward by most of the Scottish nobility. The foundation of a successful insurrection is often handed to rebels when their opponents underestimate the threats before them; the British mercenaries at Trenton in 1776, the French at Dien Bien Phu, the Ysterspruit ambush of British forces by General Koos de la Rey.

At this point Warenne must have become confused between the known, established medieval order of organised battle and a running battle with irregular native forces with limited oversight. His world was turned upside down as he faced a band of freedom fighters intent on dispatching the occupiers of Scotland. One cannot underestimate the visceral power of a group of men bound by a great common cause that is absent from their traditional foes, who are seeking to invade for enrichment – resulting in pools of blood in the Forth River at Stirling Bridge. Wallace summarily dismissed the English entreaties resulting in a quick, perhaps premature, attack across the bridge by a force led by Cressingham. That Stirling Bridge no longer exists today but research is believed to have uncovered evidence of the original bridge a short distance away from the present replica, in the river.

The historian Walter of Guisborough, recorded the English and Scottish force in the many tens of thousands but logical review suggests that these numbers defy belief. The likely size of the Warenne army was probably 5,000–10,000 foot soldiers and a few hundred cavalry, with Wallace commanding perhaps one half of that number. Prior to the start of battle there was some debate among the English leadership of differing knowledge and experience as to the best course of action other than the slow and precarious movement of troops across a narrow bridge. A suggestion for the mounted troops to cross further up the river and flank their opponents was rejected on the basis as this would split and reduce the size of the main column.

Warenne was no Hannibal and has been variously described by historical records as incapable, a blunderer, repulsive, stupid, a disastrous commander and pusillanimous. He had one very large card in his hand, a close and enduring association with King Edward based on solid, loyal service through several wars and decades. Warenne was a seasoned soldier but his experience was of no consequence in the fog of hubris.

A guerrilla and government commander have historically come from different origins although many a guerrilla commander came to the fore after government training and experience, often in colonial pre-independence armies. In medieval times and more recently in Latin America, commanders could receive appointments for loyalty or from connections, not ability, and it is in that singular predominant fact that capable guerrilla leaders arise from a meritocracy of leadership with oversight. Careless guerrillas are killed and thoughtless ones often captured. The iron discipline of ideologically driven guerrillas with a cadre of leadership given not only powers of life and death but command manoeuvrability lead to large and small successes.

Cressingham, the money counter, moved across the small Forth Bridge, leading perhaps 5,000 men and cavalry in a slow traverse that took several hours eagerly watched by William Wallace, Andrew Murray and several thousand of what are commonly called in NATO speak today, insurgents. As some point during this advance, led by a noble used to the orderly placement of soldiers on a field of battle, William, future guardian of Scotland, struck.

The column was interspersed with all the commanders including Warenne, who did not cross the bridge, Cressingham and the renowned Yorkshire knight, Marmaduke Thweng, who was the only one to come out of the forthcoming fracas with honour intact. Although accounts differ, the Scots main thrust was directed to the north-eastern end of the bridge, which had a triple effect. The blocking of the bridge prevented reinforcement, the manoeuvre split the English force and immediately demoralised those stranded in Scottish-controlled Scotland. Scottish pikemen were initially repulsed by the horse soldiers led by Marmaduke Thweng, who rallied his remaining men and forced his way back across the bridge. However the tide of battle turned against the army of Longshanks in a matter of minutes and the English force fled the field of battle.

Another common thread of guerrilla warfare is to pick the place of battle, straight out of Sun Tzu, then strike quickly, preferably at an isolated target with the ability to retreat in an equally rapid manner to protected territory.

Several hundred men of the routed English forces escaped by swimming across the Forth and one knight is even reported to have ridden into the river in full armor and swam across with his horse. The death toll was in the thousands as no quarter was given to those trapped on the Scottish side of the bridge and no effort was or could have been made to rescue them. Warenne was sufficiently concerned that he had the bridge destroyed where possible and set alight to prevent chase but the returning groups and wagons nevertheless faced continuous attack by emboldened Scottish marauders.

A guerrilla leader who woos the local populace for a **support network** also has to inspire support with victories large and small. Conversely when faced with a barbaric government, who indulge in increasingly extreme crimes against their populace, the government will also see significant acts of violence directed at their commanders and civilian administration. Often in the nature of reprisal, it also acts as a chilling reminder to rank and file that no betrayal will be countenanced upon severe penalty, often death and dismemberment. This treatment would also be meted out to the leader's own guerrillas who seek to mutiny or join a rival leader. In the late 1930s, Mao Zedong had several thousand officers and men of his own army executed for just such behaviour in the town of Futien.

The second highest English official in Scotland, Sir Hugh de Cressingham, was killed and Wallace is reputed to have taken a length of skin off Cressingham's body from head to toe, which he later used as his baldrick or sword belt.

Wallace proceeded to have a string of military victories unimpeded by the threat of a large English force, the first of which was his original target, Dundee. The English garrison, fearful after the Scottish victory, at Stirling Bridge capitulated immediately and fled south back to England. As Wallace succeeded on the battlefield, so he generated supplies and arms from the capture of English war booty resulting in a growing and self-sustaining rebel army acquiring control of larger areas of territory. Wallace then went on to secure Berwick and Edinburgh before moving south to pillage the northern English countryside until the winter weather forced his return to Scotland. It was at this time he was knighted and made guardian of Scotland.

King Edward was determined to once again impose English order on a Scotland that was now entirely controlled by the Scottish and so that spring he directed his nobles to the walled city of York to plan a punitive expedition to Scotland under Warenne, the Earl of Surrey. The Scottish nobility, for fear of Wallace or energised by the successful rebellion, mostly did not attend. A large army, numbered in the tens of thousands, was assembled with cavalry and included a new weapon of war, the longbow with metal-piercing arrows. This army moved north and easily occupied southern Scotland before taking Berwick without any significant clashes with the forces of Wallace who shadowed them in the not unreasonable expectation that the countryside, stripped of supplies, would not support such a large force.

At this point, in early summer, Edward hastily concluded a peace treaty with the French and returned to England to take command of his army.

Wallace had thus far carried on a classic guerrilla campaign by avoiding a superior force and allowing the depletion of their supplies waiting for an opportunity of his choosing to present itself. Edward had meantime ordered several supply ships up the Forth to keep his army in the field but delay meant he would have to retreat to Edinburgh. It was only then that he was informed Wallace was encamped near Callendar Wood, close to Falkirk.

Wallace had taken up a relatively safe position with a large forest to his back and a marsh to his front while facing a significantly superior force, but he also confronted several other evils at that time. The English invasion by Longshanks had caused a lack of confidence in his troops and the desertion of most of the nobility from the nationalist cause; his army was smaller by a wide margin; there was the new threat of the longbow which launched armour-piercing arrows over a longer distance than previously; and most importantly, he broke the cardinal rule of guerrilla warfare by engaging a larger, better equipped foe in a static battle.

Wallace deployed his most significant anti-cavalry weapon, the schiltron, a large circular mass of men holding long spears or pikes (often bound by ropes), similar in appearance to a giant hedgehog and designed to repel horse-borne fighters.

There were four schiltrons, that formed a line parallel to the forest and marsh, interspersed with archers. The English cavalry charged but could not penetrate the schiltron whereupon they attacked the Scottish archers who retreated. King Edward then engaged his significant force of longbowmen, who rained arrows down on

1929 statue of William Wallace, in front of the gates at Edinburgh Castle. (Ad Meskens/Wikimedia Commons)

the soldiers trapped within the schiltron with no protection from above. As casualties mounted, gaps appeared and the horsemen rushed through these openings to massacre a large number of Scots. Eventually the rest of the Scots turned and fled with William Wallace.

In only a single year, guerrilla leader William Wallace saw his rebel army dismantled, his military gains erased, his country re-occupied, his honours removed and exile to France his only avenue of escape.

These ashes have been raked over for centuries but it remains a fact that when confronted by such a superior force with extended supply lines at a static position the only option, outside of political considerations, is retreat, harassment and attrition.

Wallace eventually returned to Scotland where he was deceived and captured in 1305 by some of his own countrymen and handed over to King Edward. Edward submitted Wallace to extreme acts of public torture: for treason he was dragged upon a hurdle to the place of execution; for murder and robbery he was hung for a certain time by the neck; for burning religious houses he was removed from the gallows while alive, had his entrails removed and burnt in front of him before being quartered and his body parts dispersed.

CHAPTER 2

GENERAL GEORGE WASHINGTON, UNITED STATES OF AMERICA

Until his unconventional victory at Trenton in December 1776, the military leader of the recently created United States of America had incurred a series of losses both on the battlefield and of political confidence in his leadership, most just after the declaration of independence on 4 July 1776.

Shortly thereafter, the first and largest battle of the war against the British took place in August in Brooklyn, New York, also called the battle of Long Island, that saw the Revolutionary Army bested by a professional force led by experienced and determined officers. The British army had been an established professional force for several centuries, its ability proven in many wars being a formidable force facing a ragtag army of farmers and such it was natural that overconfidence prevailed in the war of the American Revolution.

A large British force – in the tens of thousands – invaded from the sea moving up from Staten Island to Manhattan where Washington was encamped in defence of what was an important port city. Washington was outnumbered in manpower and severely disadvantaged in artillery, but in that event it was strategy not firepower that determined the outcome of battle.

Throughout the American Revolution the captors of Revolutionary Army soldiers were surprised to discover not soldiers but farmers, sailors and tailors. George Washington was no novice when it came to the arts of war, having derived significant military experience as an officer with the Virginia militia during the French and Indian War. In addition, he spent his early life as a surveyor in the vast wilds of Virginia and Pennsylvania which gave him a comprehensive understanding of geography with experience in the interpretation of landscapes. This would provide an invaluable tool in the coming years.

The use of guerrilla tactics at Trenton was not the first time that the nascent Revolutionary Army had deployed this strategy. In April 1775, the British sought to raid a colonial store of weapons at Concord in Massachusetts but were ambushed by a small band of rebels before reaching Lexington. The raiding party continued onto Concord but failed in their objective of seizing supplies, whereupon they withdrew back to Boston. The columns of British soldiers faced continuous sniping and ambushes all the way back to Boston when the city was put under a siege by the rebel army. This was more a spontaneous response by an inferior group faced with a large professional army. The British were beginning to experience a taste of nationalist resistance armies of colonial power, something they would come up against in larger doses throughout their declining empire in the twentieth century.

A comparable event in more recent history would have been the decimation of the French GM 100 regiment shortly after the debacle at Dien Bien Phu in June 1954 as they sought to withdraw to Pleiku through the Mang Yang Pass in the central highlands of Vietnam. The Viet Minh repeatedly attacked the convoy, resulting in the loss of most equipment as well as hundreds killed, wounded and captured. When confronted by a force of foreign invaders larger in numbers, well supplied and technologically superior, commonly referred today as asymmetric warfare, a nationalist or rebel force can only resort to the ultimate tool in the toolbox: ruthlessness in pursuit of annihilation without limit as to extremity or time. This is a strategy that will demoralise the enemy, and intimidate friend and foe alike while creating political dissent back home as the dead arrive on their shores.

Trenton was a real guerrilla action in which a military leader, classically trained, sought to strike against a fixed military position, which in the military genre of mobile guerrilla warfare, would have

Washington Crossing the Delaware. (The Metropolitan Museum of Art/ Gift of John Stewart Kennedy, 1897)

resulted in retreat if faced with firm opposition or capture of the target. George Washington chose a plan to be implemented in a manner and at a time not seen before in the conflict. It was destined to catch the opposing elite force of German mercenaries by surprise and eventually inflict complete defeat of the Hessians. The plan was simple in concept. The movement of several thousand soldiers to face an encamped enemy half their number, at night, on a public holiday – Christmas Day – accompanied by three times the artillery compliment of the target, in the dead of winter, going across a swift, wide, ice ridden river.

The object of the attack was a detachment of German mercenaries fighting for the British during the revolutionary war – it being an easier recruitment by money than attempting conscription of Englishmen. They were called Hessians as they originated from the German state of Hesse-Kassel in central Germany and formed part of a military tradition of small German states with private armies for hire. They made up a substantial part of the British army during the Revolutionary War numbering in the tens of thousands with most from Hesse-Kassel. At the time of the attack the Hessians were under strength, poorly supplied with a significant number suffering from sickness. Despite this, they were still an elite and well-trained unit with high discipline, which served them well, preventing complete annihilation as events unfolded.

The place of attack was the sparsely populated town of Trenton, which had several roads leading to it across open countryside making it vulnerable to attack from many directions which the Hessian commander Rall sought to forestall with regular patrols. Whilst they had several artillery pieces and had discussed strategic placement from a protected emplacement, this was never actioned. Rall also had a regiment of several hundred always on alternate standby which had their function depleted by false alarms, poor weather and little sleep. Today, this would have been called a quick reaction force.

Washington had all this information from a network of spies spread throughout British-controlled territory including Trenton. The necessary elements were in place for a classic guerrilla action that has been regularly repeated over the years, both before and since Trenton.

The object of the attack was a static element within rebel-friendly territory, that afforded accurate intelligence on troop numbers, armament, positions, morale and movements to the commander. More recent examples of this type of attack were the frequent attacks by FARC guerrillas on the rural police stations and isolated pacification outposts of the Colombian government which were often undertaken in poor weather to prevent aerial support.

The opposing soldiers were not colonial subjects and were unlikely to receive support from the local residents, who would support any attack or uprising. The Hessians were considered the lowest, being mercenary and often brutal in their actions on and off the battlefield. Parallels can be drawn with any foreign incursion in an independence or internecine struggle such as Vietnam, Angola or Afghanistan.

The date of the attack was significant – a day when forces, particularly of the Christian faith, would be at their lowest efficiency, even conservative Germans. The weather, being winter conditions, provided cover of movement, approach and attack right up to the doors of barracks and along streets in preparation for artillery positions and troop placement.

Washington had his force of over two thousand men and 18 pieces of artillery mustered at dusk on Christmas Eve to begin a night

The battle of Trenton. (Anne S. K. Brown Military Collection, Brown University Library)

crossing of the Delaware River, from Pennsylvania into British-held New Jersey across a flowing waterway beset with large floes of ice that could crush or sink a boat. Among the many vessels utilised for the event were long, shallow draft Durham boats capable of carrying many tons of cargo, crewed by Massachusetts sailors from Marblehead. The insurgent commander had his artillery chief, the able Colonel Henry Knox, marshal the crossing as he went ahead with the first boats across the Delaware intending a sunrise attack.

Various delays including worsening weather saw the force across, but nine miles north of Trenton in the early morning. Washington nevertheless pursued the attack and divided his force into east and west elements for an encompassing attack on the slothful but still dangerous Hessians. A modern corollary of this event might be the Herculean movement of several hundred dissembled artillery pieces uphill in a tropical environment by Viet Minh General Vo Nguyen Giap in March 1954 to rain steel on the French defenders of Dien Bien Phu, who were reduced to airlift and parachute supplies under fire. Unlike Washington, Giap had to occupy the surrounding hills to secure artillery positions before the siege could begin but similar

Heavy and slow **artillery** have not generally formed part of the guerrilla arsenal but instead have been used and discarded after capture as part of an overall strategy or retained if desired for the rare occasions of securing base territory gathering points. Over time, artillery has been replaced by the ubiquitous rocket-propelled grenade, wire-guided anti-tank mobile missile or shoulder fired anti-aircraft missile and more recently by vehicle-borne explosive devices.

to Washington, the cannon fire carried the day. There are also similarities with the South African Defence Force's attack on the besieged Angolan and Cuban troops at Cuito Cuanavale in 1987, except there was no eventual surrender or retreat.

The Trenton attack force had a key commander in Colonel Henry Knox, who secured the crossing of men and cannon before proceeding to Trenton where artillery was strategically placed and moved, when necessary, to command the open streets. Hessians were neither unable to form up for a significant counter-attack or reduce themselves to small roving irregular bands under the Germanic military theory prevailing at that time.

On 26 December 1776, Washington led his men to the first encounter with a Hessian outpost, a mile from Trenton, where there was an exchange of gunfire before they fled to Trenton to warn their companions of the American assault. Washington dispersed his men and cannon at key points, especially at King and Queen Streets which was ironic not only because of the name, but also because that was the very spot Rall had contemplated establishing an artillery emplacement. The disciplined Hessians repeatedly retreated, returning fire and receiving cover fire from other soldiers as they went towards the north end of Trenton.

Colonel Rall, who took command after some delay, formed up his men to come up the streets to overcome the rebel artillery but this failed at every attempt due to the volume of fire from the American rebels and even fire from some citizenry from the protection of buildings along the open streets. The Hessians then

The battle of Trenton. (Anne S. K. Brown Military Collection, Brown University Library)

faced an overwhelming attack of men, musket shot and cannon fire which led to the capture and abandonment of the Hessian cannons forcing a full retreat to the rising open field to the north of Trenton where Rall formed up his men in lines to counter-attack. Some Hessians fled the area completely in a wild attempt to reach safety and evade capture.

Washington repulsed this attack, during which Rall was critically wounded. The Hessians broke and fled to a nearby orchard having incurred about a hundred casualties, which only further demoralised them as they faced abject defeat in North America for the first time. German descendant and German-speaking members of Washington's raiding party shouted out to the Hessians to surrender, which they eventually did in acknowledgement of the futility of further conflict. The captives were nearly a thousand in number with a dead commander, many dead officers and all their arms, artillery and supplies being seized by the rebel army.

Washington had made his first victory for 1776, which started a reversal of fortune for the British that ended at Yorktown in 1781 with the aid of French assistance to the American Revolution. Those who regard the liberation of France in 1944 as a feat undertaken without French assistance and because of French defeatism should remember the French aid received during the American War of

Surrender of Hessian soldiers at the battle of Trenton (Anne S. K. Brown Military Collection, Brown University Library)

Revolution. The sight of a thousand defeated Hessians marching through Pennsylvania to Philadelphia (and sometimes deserting to the rebel cause) was great propaganda for a conscript army in much need of aid, far more valuable than an unseen battlefield of dead Hessians.

The guerrilla leader must pursue military success, large and small, enjoin the support of the local populace, control territory not in the classic sense, but in a widely dispersed manner by road blocks, kidnappings, attacks on government buildings and seizing every opportunity for a propaganda victory. This does not exclude the widespread use of kangaroo courts and spontaneous executions to instill fear and discipline often in the early part of an insurgency or when the inevitable social programmes of education, medical assistance, food and ideology are not sufficient carrot. Many Hessians, in the thousands, were convinced to remain in America during and after the war with offers of land and the entreaties of their distant German relatives who now lived and prospered not as peasants but land owners and tradesmen. The feudal system was in the last stages of extinction. This paradigm was later seen at Dien Bien Phu when the surrounded French army faced a determined Viet Minh, who could have ordered their destruction but chose the higher and longer value of surrender.

The success at Trenton led Washington to engage the British shortly after for two successive and successful encounters that eventually caused the Redcoats to retreat from southern New Jersey.

Upon hearing news of the defeat of the Hessians, Lord Cornwallis gathered a force of several thousand men and moved south towards Trenton from New York in early January 1777. At Princeton, he detached over a thousand men under Lieutenant-Colonel Mawhood from the army to act as a rearguard and to control Princeton. The British column then moved towards Trenton where they encountered a forward unit of the Revolutionary Army which repeatedly attacked them causing delay, often as they tried to form up in a classic manner, against what was a strategic series of hopping guerrilla ambushes. Hindsight victorious, had the British kept moving and even accelerated their pace to Trenton in recognition of this delaying tactic by Washington, the outcome – of a force almost double the number of their foes – may have been different.

At Trenton, Washington placed his men south along the Assunpink Creek, a tributary of the Delaware, with most massed at the only bridge, to create a choke point and in modern terms, a kill zone. The harassing attacks slowed the Cornwallis advance and the vanguard column reached the bridge in the afternoon, making an unsuccessful attack to take the bridge. The poor light of dusk on the field of battle greeted a now reluctant Cornwallis who decided to call off operations until the next morning. Here a great similarity appears with the guerrilla strategy of William Wallace, who repelled the British at Stirling Bridge using geography, local knowledge and intelligence to the best advantage. Another well-worn lesson would be that on being confronted by a superior army, force them into a choke point to turn a large group into the width of the restricting element and thereby manageable numbers for the lesser group of defenders. An example of this would be the stairways of some old slave plantation houses that narrow at the top, constricting access and allowing more concentrated use of a blunderbuss or shotgun.

Battle of Princeton. (Anne S. K. Brown Military Collection, Brown University Library)

That night, Washington and his force moved north under the cover of subterfuge noises and fires to fool Cornwallis into thinking that the Americans were encamped, also awaiting battle the next day. This second victory was a mere seven days after the destruction of the Hessians on Boxing Day and proved that in matters military, hubris creates a mirage of success.

In a version of never letting the right hand know what the left is doing or keep the enemy guessing, it is important for the success of guerrilla actions that they employ military deception, telegraphing several possible positions or strategies to prevent an enemy from seizing on the core tactic.

Washington and his band of revolutionaries went quietly towards Princeton running parallel to Assunpink Creek which he crossed before continuing along a frozen road, the ice helping to move his artillery. A forward party led by Brigadier General Mercer sent ahead to secure the bridge over Stony Brook soon encountered a part of Mawhood's force from Princeton, whereupon the Redcoats immediately attacked and overwhelmed Mercer who was killed and cannons captured.

Many guerrilla leaders often pursue a pattern of distant command to officers in the field, Fidel Castro among them, but in some situations, **obvious and open leadership** is required, such as displayed by William Wallace, Koos de la Rey and Manuel Marulanda of the Colombian FARC. A leader by his manner whether humble or bombastic must use his character or presence to unify his command as distinct from leadership troikas or groups who rely on the power of the group and not individual charisma. This would be an inspiration to a rebel army who feed on thoughts more often than food; who embrace charismatic leadership more powerful than ammunition and receive confidence from a military leader surrounded by competent commanders equally brave, rather than a personality cult. Examples of the latter would be Jonas Savimbi of Angola and the failed leader of the Tamil insurrection in Sri Lanka, Velupillai Prabhakaran.

Washington came upon the fleeing remnants and immediately pressed an attack that forced Mawhood's retreat with many casualties and loss of equipment. General Washington had charged the British line at the head of his insurgent force and held fire until close enough. In the ensuing confusion, some thought Washington killed, but it was not so and his reputation – in ashes a week earlier – now soared.

Mawhood tried to hold the marauding American rebel contingent at several points on the approach to Princeton but eventually retreated with some of his soldiers and holed up at his base in Nassau Hall, today the oldest building in Princeton University, before several volleys of American rebel cannon fire forced the surrender of nearly two hundred of Her Majesty's finest.

Apart from the significant numbers of prisoners the American rebels were able to seize supplies, much-needed artillery and scarce supplies in a winter wilderness. The British suffered nearly three hundred wounded and killed whilst the aggressive Washington counted losses of little over a third of that number.

Battle of Princeton. (Anne S. K. Brown Military Collection, Brown University Library)

Casualties are a major part of any guerrilla agenda when an asymmetric struggle requires the parsimonious management of resources by a guerrilla leader. A guerrilla campaign inevitably involves a small locally supported force facing a larger force with all the assets of an entrenched government or occupier necessitating the use of small, well-planned actions that limit the potential loss of soldiers. A guerrilla war that can go on for years or decades sees the push and pull as territory is seized, reclaimed and then lost again. This pendulum tactic is also applicable to battles, where guerrillas limit exposure of the few against the many, and was successfully deployed by Washington at Trenton, Second Trenton and Princeton. It is arguable whether the war of the American Revolution would have continued for another four years had Washington not reverted to his classic training of stand and fight.

Between Trenton and Princeton, Washington's army had taken nearly 1,500 British prisoners and inflicted almost 400 casualties while limiting their own losses to only a hundred, which was a significant achievement against the backdrop of the Revolutionary

A **disciplined guerrilla leader** knows when to move forward or recede like the tide taking a little bit of a time, not only swimming among the fishes as prescribed by Mao on the Long March but nibbling like fish at a much larger object. Rebel commanders are instinctively closer to their men than institutional officers and are more aware and responsive to their needs.

Army performance to that time. Statistics compiled in 1875 by the U.S. Surgeon-General have British losses at 25,481 against 7,883 American losses during the entire conflict with the majority of Redcoat deaths coming in battles after Trenton.

Cornwallis, having been alerted by Mawhood as to the American deception, proceeded to march back to Princeton to not only attack Washington but to prevent a rebel attack on his base at New Brunswick where, among other things, the pay chest for his troops was being held. Washington held a council to consider the temptation of the New Brunswick prize but was convinced to hold on to their successive victories to date and retire to Morristown to the north and wait out the rest of the winter. Cornwallis eventually withdrew his outlying troops to New Brunswick and the Revolutionary War was paused for several months.

The camp at Morristown was not only a reward for fine work enabling enjoyment of the spoils of war but also allowed rest after exhausting marches and little food. The location at Morristown was close enough, just over twenty miles, to keep an eye on Cornwallis but far enough that Washington could manoeuvre upon prompt intelligence from his wide-ranging local sources, many of them recent converts to the cause as Washington's victories had made the revolution somewhat more viable.

A short time after, in 1778, France officially recognised the United States as a country and although it had been quietly supplying the rebel army for many years, it now openly supported the American Revolution with arms, supplies and soldiers. This alliance became the tipping point for the British occupation of the United States

The British surrendering their arms to General Washington after the defeat at Yorktown, Virginia, October 1781. (Anne S. K. Brown Military Collection, Brown University Library)

leading up to the French-American victory at Yorktown in 1781, which saw the surrender of the British commander and several thousand Redcoats.

Strategic alliances are the backbone of many a military success story and often they make strange bedfellows to the untutored eye. France had an axe to grind from their loss in the Seven Years' War several decades earlier – when France had ceded territory in North America and elsewhere – which gave it much incentive to aid the young rebel army. Similar alliances have occurred over the centuries; Germany and the Boers of South Africa, China and USSR with Vietnam, Cuba and the FARC of Colombia, USA and South Africa for UNITA in Angola, India and the LTTE of Sri Lanka. In many cases these alliances can last several decades and are most often surreptitious in nature but on rare occasions there can be a parting of ways such as the short border war between China and Vietnam in 1979. The United States has had an enduring friendship with France in the centuries since the Revolution, culminating with American forces coming to the belated rescue of France from Nazi occupation in June 1944.

Cornwallis resigning sword to Washington in 1781. (Anne S. K. Brown Military Collection, Brown University Library)

George Washington went on to become the first president of the newly independent United States of America, an accolade that has escaped many guerrilla leaders. In this he displayed the ultimate and necessary characteristic of a great guerrilla leader, the transformation of a rebel army into an enduring democratic state that enshrined the belief that all men are created equal.

CHAPTER 3

SIMON BOLIVAR, VENEZUELA

Simon Bolivar made a successful career of failures, defeats, elimination of competing fellow countrymen and repeated exiles manifested in the numerous early short-lived republics of Venezuela. A child of Venezuela, but ultimately a citizen of Latin America, Simon Bolivar began the liberation struggle of his home country in 1808 when its Spanish rulers were distracted by the Peninsula War against the French. Like many guerrilla leaders he had the benefit of a comfortable family background, which extended into an education that included international learning and attendance at a military academy.

After a coup and unilateral declaration of independence by Venezuelan leaders in 1810, Bolivar, then a colonel, was put in charge of the fortified coastal town of Puerto Cabello in 1812. He soon lost the town to the advancing Spanish forces, in part due to the defection of his fellow commander, Francisco Vinoni. It was not an auspicious beginning for the man later referred to as El Libertador or more recently American Liberator. This period, often referred to as the First Republic of Venezuela, was led by Francisco de Miranda, who surrendered to the Spanish and was handed over to them in anger by a group led by Bolivar. Miranda never saw freedom again and died in a Spanish jail cell.

Bolivar went on to join the independence movement in the united provinces of New Granada, which approximated to

Captain General Simon Bolivar. (Iamcharles66/Wikimedia Commons)

A recurring characteristic of nationalist and guerrilla movements is the **jockeying for power among the leadership**, whereby sub-groups are formed to push a particular person or cabal into the position of ultimate leadership and maintain that appointment. Many early leaders of the Cuban Revolution and possible future competitors to Fidel Castro soon disappeared from public view, either due to incarceration or death, including Huber Matos and Camilo Cienfuegos. As the saying goes it is better to be on the inside looking out than the outside looking in.

Cannon exhibit, Cucuta, Colombia. (Ricardocolombia/Wikimedia Commons)

modern-day Colombia, Venezuela, Ecuador and Panama, before it was put down by Spanish forces in 1816. During this period of his life, Bolivar successfully attacked and captured several towns and cities before being granted permission to continue the Venezuelan liberation movement.

The road to Venezuelan independence – and confirmation that Bolivar was a capable military leader – began in the little known, or remembered, Colombian town of Cucuta that lay just west of the Venezuela border. Ordered to attack an 800-strong force of Spanish soldiers under General Ramon Correa, Bolivar began to display the makings of a guerrilla leader when he came upon the Spaniards guarding a high mountain pass. He responded by sending a false letter that his counterpart, Colonel Castillo, was advancing on Pamplona to the south. They deliberately allowed it to be intercepted and the Spanish force turned and left the choke point for Cucuta.

Bolivar and Castillo, with a force half the size of their target, then crossed the Zulia River and attacked Cucuta on the morning of

Zulia River, Colombia. (EEIM/Wikimedia Commons)

28 February 1813, the last Sabbath of Lent. The Spanish general was taken by surprise and rallied his troops, who fled in the face of an uphill bayonet charge ordered by Bolivar, who was not yet thirty years old. The defeated Spanish invaders suffered twenty dead soldiers and tens of wounded whereas Bolivar incurred only a tenth of that. His small but victorious army was rewarded with supplies, munitions and Bolivar was promoted to general by a grateful Colombian government in waiting.

There are significant similarities between Bolivar's action at Cucuta and Washington's at Trenton – Washington's actions were likely known by Bolivar from his studies in Spain:

1. Efforts were made to deceive the enemy, lulling them into a sense of complacency believing that either no attack was imminent or it was likely to happen elsewhere.
2. The Colombian and American forces both crossed rivers before their attack, the Zulia to the west of Cucuta and the Delaware south of Trenton.
3. Attacks were commenced on a religious day when leaders were distracted; in the case of Spanish General Correa, he was attending mass.

4. The attack was a surprise with rushed movement in a ferocious manner giving the enemy little time to consolidate.

5. It was a young and well-informed rebel force attacking foreign invaders on their home territory.

These guerrilla strategies have endured through to the recent conflicts in the present-day Middle East where entrenched governments and foreign allies seek to impose their will on a people who have risen for a revolutionary change or death. It has been mostly the latter.

The following June, in the western state of Trujillo, an empowered Bolivar famously issued a Decree of War to the Death whereby Venezuelan guerrillas were absolved of all acts of violence, murder or atrocities against Spanish citizens in Venezuela:

Venezuelans: an army of brothers, sent by the sovereign Congress of New Granada, has come to free you, and it is already amongst you, after evicting the oppressors from the provinces of Mérida and Trujillo.

We are the ones sent to destroy the Spaniards, to protect the Americans, and to reestablish the republican governments that formed the Confederation of Venezuela. The states covering our arms (weapons) are once again ruled by their old constitutions and magistrates, fully enjoying their liberty and independence; for our mission is only to break the chains of servitude, which still oppress some of our peoples, not claiming to create laws, or enforce acts of domination, which the right of war could authorise us to do.

Touched by your misfortunes, we could not indifferently watch the afflictions inflicted to you by the barbaric Spaniards, who have annihilated you with robbery and destroyed you with death, infringed the most solemn treaties and capitulations; in one word, committed every crime, reducing the Republic of Venezuela to the most horrific desolation. It is so that justice demands vindication, and necessity forces us to take it. May the monsters that infest Colombian soil, and have covered it with blood disappear for good; may their punishment be equal to the magnitude of their treason, so that the stain of our ignominy is washed off, and to show the nations of the universe that the sons of America cannot be offended without punishment.

In spite of our just resentments against the iniquitous Spaniards, our magnanimity still deigns itself to open, for the last time, a route to conciliation and friendship; we still invite them to live peacefully among us, if, hating their crimes and turning to good faith, they cooperate with us in the destruction of the intruding government of Spain, and the reestablishment of the Republic of Venezuela.

All Spaniards who do not conspire against tyranny in favour of our just cause, using the most effective and active resources, will be considered enemies, and will be punished as traitors to the homeland, and therefore, will be promptly executed. On the other hand, a general and absolute pardon is issued to all Spaniards who pass into our army, with or without their weapons; to those who offer aid to the good citizens working hard to shake off the shackles of tyranny. War officers and magistrates that proclaim the government of Venezuela and join our cause will keep their destinies and work positions; in one word, all Spaniards who perform service for the State will be reputed and treated as Americans.

And you, Americans, who have been separated from the road of justice by error and perfidy, know that your brothers forgive you and seriously regret your misdeeds, intimately persuaded that you cannot be guilty, and that only the ignorance and blindness imposed on you by the authors of your crimes could cause you to perpetrate them. Do not fear the sword that comes to avenge you and cut the ignominious bindings which tie you to your executioners' fate. Rely on absolute immunity for your honour, life and properties; the mere title of Americans will be you warranty and safeguard. Our weapons have come to protect you, and will never be used against a single one of our brothers.

This amnesty extends to the very traitors who have most recently committed their acts of felony; and will be so religiously carried out that no reason, cause or pretext will be enough to make us break our offer, no matter how extraordinary the reasons you give us to excite our adversity.

Spaniards and Canarians, count on death, even if indifferent, if you do not actively work in favour of the independence of America. Americans, count on life, even if guilty.

Today this would be cause for an International Criminal Court prosecution for genocide. This was when the scion of an upper-class

The **International Criminal Court** was created in 2002 by the Rome Statute of the United Nations. It has undertaken prosecutions on the charge of genocide against convicted Serbian and African leaders but facilitators of the earlier unlawful detention of political opponents, many of whom succumbed to disease or death in Africa, the Caribbean, Malaya and Kenya, have escaped punishment while still walking among us.

family conservative in his views became not only a guerrilla in the true meaning, but a ruthless leader who prepared his followers to make the ultimate sacrifice for their cause and instill widespread fear in the enemy.

Conquest massacres were not a new phenomenon of the time, having been pioneered throughout the New World by Spanish adventurers and conquistadors, who decimated native Indians with wild abandon, often by importation of disease. Early independence movements felt the hard toe of Spanish oppression with executions, incarcerations or simple exile, covering their actions by the thin veneer of government authority and judicial executions.

One, possibly unforeseen, significance of the decree lay in its adoption by future generations of rebels spinning Bolivar's message so that violence and extrajudicial killings became a necessary part of any liberation movement and by extension, a particular political ideology. Some guerrilla movements would utilise this as a manifesto of operation in their political struggles by applying this sentence to their own countrymen, writ large by the FARC insurgency from 1964. This concept has even been extended to the Venezuela of Bolivar's birth where it is the government not guerrillas who have applied this maxim against political opponents and even people in the street. Guerrilla leaders too often follow the writings and history of Bolivar, without separating wheat from the chaff, the excess of robotic adherence.

After Trujillo, Bolivar continued marching east at speed towards the capital city of Caracas as part of what became known as the Admirable campaign, with little resistance from pro-Spanish forces.

Guerrilla forces have to be sensitised to the sway of a conflict allowing them to take advantage of the smallest gain. Riding on the back of recent victories, just like Washington, Bolivar experienced increasing support and men rallying to his columns, including enemy deserters. A second and perhaps more important reason is that the inevitable poorly supplied guerrilla army with limited logistical support must make haste while supplies, and most necessary, indigenous support is at a high. At all times in the caravan to Caracas, Bolivar was aware of the threat of large pro-Spanish forces in neighbouring provinces, but he kept his eye on the prize.

In what became a characteristic of his guerrilla leadership and a bane to his enemies, Bolivar suddenly reversed course to go south to attack Barinas where a large pro-Spanish force was encamped. Although an arduous journey over a mountain range, Bolivar was rewarded by an enemy that fled the city leaving supplies and munitions for the rebel army. Mao Zedong adopted similar tactics on the Long March in 1934–35 and even crossed the same river four times to confuse his pursuers. There was some risk in this manoeuvre by Bolivar to what was a small rebel column in transit to the capital city changing course to engage an enemy-occupied city on a plain with other forces in nearby provinces. Fortune favours the brave.

This was another victory that enhanced the stature of the movement, which was not all war but speeches and writings that encouraged support while threatening retaliation for those falling short. It was a template that would be followed by nearly every future Latin American rebel leader. Another facet pioneered by Bolivar was proclaiming better rights for the underclass of Creoles or Pardos who, sensing an opportunity for social and economic advancement, threw their support and lives behind the cause.

Bolivar then made his final advance on Caracas, a city in confusion as government officials fled with no significant military defences available. He arrived at an open city on 6 August 1813, El Libertador. Celebrations commenced with a parade accompanied by flowers, young girls in white and church bells after which Bolivar declared the Second Republic of Venezuela. It was not to last.

Renewed support from Spain for a rising pro-Spanish leader, Jose Tomas Boves, shortly after Bolivar entered Caracas, forced a series of battles in outlying provinces of Venezuela that decimated the country of people and prosperity. Boves came from the wild, periodically flooded, llanos of Venezuela and enjoyed the support of the llaneros who were rewarded by seized land and possessions as they fought battle after battle. Boves' success was exacerbated by Bolivar's failure to free slaves, thus weakening the previous rebel, now government, army, as Bolivar moved west of Caracas to his estate at San Mateo. A threatened encirclement forced Bolivar to flee further west. He left some of his army behind; it was overwhelmed and many were killed. There is a school of thought that Bolivar sought to protect the family hacienda from a marauding pro-Spain force led by the ruthless Boves and another that he sought to draw them away from Caracas.

Bolivar continued to retreat, looting churches of their valuables as he went, while facing a continuous series of defeats that resulted in the end of the Second Republic and his departure from Venezuela. He sailed to Cartagena, Colombia in September 1814 where the sitting government made him captain-general before setting him to defend the federation of New Granada and pursue essentially Colombian ambitions. This lasted until he lay siege to Cartagena when infighting among local factions forced him to flee again, this time to Jamaica in May 1815, where he wrote his famous Carta de Jamaica or Jamaica Letter. In the letter, he sought to review his past history and the necessity of a union among countries of the Americas. By the following December having endured poverty, refusal of British aid, and an assassination attempt, he made his way to Haiti to seek support for an invasion of Venezuela.

In Haiti, Bolivar received support from President Alexandre Petion for several months, but he had to promise that any venture to Venezuela would include the abolition of slavery. After receiving material and military support from the Haitian government, Bolivar sailed back to Venezuela in April 1816 but failure caused him to return and in September 1816, he again returned to Venezuela. Haitian assistance was a most timely and crucial gesture when the independence of Venezuela appeared to be passing into myth and not

A trait among guerrilla leaders is to attempt to maintain **friendly relations with nations on the border of their area of operations** to facilitate not only a line of logistical support but a protected area in the event of retreat. This was certainly the case of the FARC of Colombia who would utilise the sparsely populated areas of the border with Venezuela in an attempt to avoid the targeted bombings on their leadership by the Colombian Army. The important distinction lay in avoiding too much heat for the host country or becoming involved in their local politics causing the withdrawal of the welcome mat.

When faced with overwhelming odds and possible decimation, a guerrilla leader will often flee into the arms of political asylum in hopes of being able to fight another day. The host nation will, in return, have a card to play with the country of origin and often receive concessions that can be sufficiently large to encourage the detention or disappearance of the guerrilla leader in waiting. An example of this was the May 1984 La Penca bombing assassination attempt on Eden Pastora at the Nicaragua and Costa Rican border, which killed several journalists but not Commandante Cero.

reality, regrettably unremembered in her poor economic state today by the Bolivarean republics. 1817 found Bolivar and his small force from Haiti coming up the Orinoco River to Angostura, now Ciudad Bolivar, in central Venezuela where he joined General Manuel Piar who had laid siege to the city for several months and helped to capture the city. The experienced and successful Piar was quickly sidelined before Bolivar had him executed in September 1817.

In Angostura, in 1818, Bolivar began publication of the widely read *Correo del Orinoco*, the oldest newspaper in Latin America today. It was the media outlet for the Venezuelan rebels and their nearby aspirants. Again, an outstanding strategic move, though not original, as it joined a long line of pamphlets, posters and news sheets that have promoted the cause of freedom for small and large groups throughout the ages. Published propaganda was an avenue often used to sculpt the minds of citizens, many of whom were

A recurring pathos of guerrilla leaders is the irresistible **urge to murder competitors**, often overly competent fellow commanders, chief among them Jonas Savimbi, who regularly purged his ranks causing many defections that culminated in his downfall. Geraldo Sachipengo (Nunda), general in UNITA and later the head of the Angolan army, narrowly escaped with his life before defecting to help in the successful hunt for Savimbi. Another modern example would be the execution of a hero of the Cuban revolution and Angola, General Arnaldo Ochoa Sanchez, who was murdered by the Cuban state in July 1989 after many internationalist military tours. He was a popular military leader whose widespread regard eventually became a death sentence.

General Manuel Carlos Piar. (Wikimedia Commons)

Ciudad, Bolivar, formerly Angostura, 2009. (Daniel Lopez Monagas (Zokeber)/Wikimedia Commons)

illiterate, receiving the news from readers or word of mouth. The social network revolution has irreversibly changed that paradigm.

It was in Angostura that Bolivar began to consolidate his power among the anti-Spain forces by being elected president at their second congress in February 1819 before preparing to start a series of battles to establish the independence of New Granada. As part of this initiative, Bolivar recruited several thousand former veteran soldiers and officers of the Napoleonic wars under the banner of the British or Albion Legion (although it included Irish and German mercenaries as well). A tried and true formula for any guerrilla leader is to make friends with the enemies of the prevailing government. At that time, these soldiers were among the poor and dispossessed with nothing to look forward to back home.

The son of the Llanos, Jose Tomas Boves, was killed at the battle of Urica in December 1814, which led to the gradual dissipation of his llanero force, with many of them later joining Bolivar in his campaign of 1819 under Jose Paez. It was a significant boost to Bolivar's latest attempt at a rebel army with increased prospects of success with the size and experience of his soldiers and commanders.

The opening salvo of another march to independence took place near the town of Paipa in the province or department of Boyaca of Colombia some distance from the border with Venezuela, which become known as the Vargas Swamp battle on 25 July 1819. Bolivar's troops crossed a mountainous region and swamp, before being initially repelled by the Spanish forces on a hill, but were

Lancers monument, Paipa, Colombia, 2006. (Kamilokardona/Wikimedia Commons)

saved by two salutary actions. An uphill charge by the experienced Irish commander of the British Legion, James Rooke, overtook Spanish positions and turned the tide. That hill, later named War Hill, saw Rooke dying from his battle wounds but expressing a wish to be buried in the new South America.

The final coup de grace came in the form of fourteen llanero lancers, led by Juan Jose Rondon, who turned the pro-Spanish forces' resistance into a retreat. This significant act of heroism was recorded by a magnificent sculpture in 1970 depicting the fourteen horsemen in full flight located near Paipa.

Bolivar's army and other Spanish forces, both in the low thousands, then began a southern parallel race to what is modern-day Bogota in an effort to seize control of this politically and strategically important junction with little defensive strength. Less than two weeks later, on 7 August 1819, Bolivar's two columns were able to block the Spanish rearguard which had become separated from its vanguard and had moved quickly to take up positions at the Boyaca Bridge. The rebels attacked the isolated rearguard, resulting in an immediate retreat and their cavalry fleeing in an

Throughout history, many guerrilla movements have encountered supporters and **participants from other countries** who believe in the struggle sufficient to join the movements in the combat zones. Apart from the British Legion who had less than altruistic motives there was Lafayette in the American Revolution, Che Guevara in Cuba, and most recently Tanja Nijmeijer in the FARC of Colombia. If the past is any guide, then once the conflict recedes, the survivors will either return home or seek another struggle to embrace.

attempt to join up with the vanguard column at the bridge. The Spanish forces commanded by Jose Barreiro were now effectively divided into three parts, all substantially reduced in number. The Spanish attempt to create a bottleneck ambush at the bridge had been defeated by a flanking rebel manoeuvre that turned obstacle to advantage. Concentrated fire stalled the cavalry while some of Bolivar's forces were able to ford the river and attack the rear of the Spanish forces that were guarding the bridge. This purpose created confusion, in effect a battle on three fronts, and caused the defeat of the Spanish column that mainly fled or surrendered in numbers reaching almost two thousand.

Boyaca joins other famous bridge-centered battles including William Wallace at Stirling Bridge and George Washington at Stony Brook Bridge during the attack on Princeton. Pro-Spanish commander Barreiro was not so lucky and was completely out-manoeuvred by Bolivar's field commanders.

The battle only lasted two hours and the Spanish commander surrendered with most of his officers including Francisco Vinoni, who had betrayed Bolivar during his first military appointment at Puerto Cabello in 1812 and which had caused Bolivar to flee in disgrace. In keeping with his prior predilections, now expanded to include former enemies, Bolivar had Vinoni hung in the square of Ventaquemada.

The guerrilla tactics used in Bolivar's campaigns included quick movement unencumbered by a large supply train; the division of the

The battle of Boyaca, Martín Tovar y Tovar. (Wikimedia Commons)

enemy force being of greater importance the more disproportionate the size of the opposing group; avoiding the bridge choke point; flanking the choke point to surprise and panic the static force; forcibly resisting any attempts at a break out or counter-attack.

Bolivar was ably supported by competent field commanders leading experienced soldiers, recently emboldened from the Vargas Swamp victory, who executed a splintering manoeuvre that ultimately caused the loss of Spanish soldiers and quashed any hope of them reaching Bogota.

This success led to Bolivar and his army entering the liberated city of Bogota on 10 August 1819, while setting the stage for an expansion of the independence conflict to create the Gran Colombia assemblage of Colombia, Venezuela, Panama and Ecuador. The pro-Spanish forces signed an armistice shortly after in November 1820 which gave them a desperately required hiatus following a string of setbacks, to include a failure to receive substantial reinforcements from Spain. As a general rule, truces are a bad idea when the invading enemy has endured a string of losses and appear to have significant problems with political support, supplies and reinforcements. One such situation was the South African and Cuban peace accord at

Boyaca Bridge in 2006. (Kamilokardona/Wikimedia Commons)

Ruacana in 1988 during the Angolan civil war in which they were both satellite participants. The debate continues today as to who was the invading force and who the rescuers.

Peace talks are a good idea for a rebel force seeking to give an appearance of transition from the bush to participation in government or civil society, as seen with the much-criticised 1999 FARC accord, which not only saw a cessation of hostilities but a significant demilitarised zone. Those few years before the breakdown of discussions saw a consolidation of FARC power in their home region and an exponential growth in numbers and supplies which ultimately allowed them to continue their struggle until 2016, seventeen long years later. The savvy FARC leader Manuel Marulanda, who had little formal education and spent his entire life in a jungle-based struggle, out-manoeuvred an entire government.

Following on from the Boyaca victory, Bolivar was successful in the battle of Carabobo in 1821 which allowed him to reclaim Caracas, see off Spanish occupation in that region permanently and finally, the establishment of the Gran Colombia collection of countries that eventually broke up into separate republics included one named after him, Bolivia. Bolivar died in 1830.

CHAPTER 4

KOOS DE LA REY, SOUTH AFRICA

Very few guerrilla leaders have had a popular song written about them nearly one hundred years after their death, but that was just the case with the Afrikaans singer Bok van Blerk's 2006 album, *de La Rey*. Boer General Jacobus Herculaas de la Rey, more popularly called Koos, a shortened Dutch form of Jacob, also widely known as Lion of the West or Western Transvaal, was memorialised by the song that attracted a groundswell of support from young South African Boers seeking a leader from the past.

Koos was born in Winburg, South Africa in 1847 to a Voortrekker or Boer pioneer family in what became the Orange Free State, once an independent Boer republic within South Africa, but today the province of Free State. His family was part of the Great Trek away from the British-controlled province of Cape Colony undertaken by Boers – which is an Afrikaans word for farmers – that led to several independent states including the Transvaal.

When he came into the world, the British and Boers were at war, leading up to the battle of Boomplaats the following year, which was recorded as a British victory. Koos' father participated in the conflict and the family farm, in keeping with British policy at the time, was confiscated and the family relocated to the Western Transvaal. Early transgressions and injustice provide a concrete platform for a lifetime of guerrilla struggle, the stamina for which will always be a continuing source of amazement and puzzlement to oppressors long after they have departed back to their countries of origin.

Many guerrilla leaders have risen from a simple background in circumstances of injustice, whether directly against them, their family or friends, just as some took to the struggle in sympathy for the downtrodden underclass. In this, Koos de la Rey was more akin to William Wallace or Manuel Marulanda of the FARC than George Washington or Simon Bolivar who emerged from privileged backgrounds.

Koos did not receive an extensive education but was raised in a tough rural environment which provided him with the many basic facets necessary for a guerrilla commander at that time and in that region. He became employed as a courier rider in Kimberley, famous for its diamond fields, which allowed him to develop skills including horse riding, local geography and surviving in an inhospitable environment. His early experiences were similar to those of other leaders including George Washington as a land surveyor in the wilds of Virginia and Pennsylvania or Manuel Marulanda as a peasant child in the mountains and jungles of Colombia.

After several years and some military experience, Koos married in 1876 and settled on a farm in Lichtenburg, north-west South Africa, a town which became famous after his death for a diamond rush in 1926. Successful farming led to his purchase of a second farm at Elandsfontein located south of Johannesburg, which stayed in the family his entire life.

Ten years before settling down, like many other Boer irregulars, Koos received his first military experience in the last of a series of low-intensity wars with the indigenous Basuto people as they fought with the Boers over land occupation ending with British intervention. He was not yet twenty years old when he took up arms for the first time and experienced the ebb and flow of a small war on the wide expanse of the South African high veld. He later went on to fight in the Sekhukhune war near the Limpopo River as the local natives under King Sekhukhune fought the Voortrekkers who had taken their land. This involved several battles and defeats for a combination of British, Boer and Swazi forces before eventual victory in 1879.

General Jacobus 'Koos' de la Rey. (Anglo-Boer War Museum)

This series of battles would have provided an attentive participant like Koos with wide experience in the combination of different forces, movement and supply of a large force in the South African environment, use of artillery and general war strategy.

His next experience was in the short First Anglo-Boer War or Transvaal War of 1880 when the British sought to suppress the aspirations of independence by the Boers of Transvaal that ultimately resulted in recognition of internal independence of the Transvaal by the British. Like many small wars, the conflict was ignited by the small act of seizure of a wagonload of wood by a British bailiff and the eruption of what had been a simmering rebellion.

Koos first appears in records as having arrested the British magistrate of Lichtenburg, suggesting he was rising in the ranks of the Boer irregular military apparatus. He then went on to be elected as a member of the Transvaal Volksraad or people's council in 1883 and commandant of Boer forces in his home town of Lichtenburg, appointments that reflected the high regard with which he was held by the local populace.

Not every guerrilla leader emerges from the near anarchy of a rebellion like William Wallace or Manuel Marulanda of the FARC, but they also arise from the steady and persistent attempt to organise an independent government with all the underlying necessary institutions such as that evolution with George Washington and Simon Bolivar.

Koos de la Rey was, like many of his compatriots, a deeply religious man, relying on the teachings and faith from the bible, not some imported abstract political theory from a distant European mind. Koos de la Rye's religious beliefs were shared by the Boers for whom he fought. This culture still exists today. The wholesale adoption of Marxist or leftist theory for a political struggle fell short in countries with an extensive Catholic population such as Colombia and Vietnam.

A significant aspect of the Boer irregular army of the time was its ability to have a large number of troops stand to, in a prompt and comprehensive fashion, upon the outbreak of any small or large conflict. This required no large logistical infrastructure as it was essentially a very large on-call local militia. Such a guerrilla army concept dates back to the days of William Wallace and continues into modern times with the successors to Washington's minutemen, the more formal National Guard of the United States.

Koos' first experience as a commander in the field was at the siege of the British fort at Potchefstroom in 1880, where he was a subordinate to General Piet Cronje – with whom he frequently disagreed. Here he developed a healthy distaste for military operations at a fixed position over an extended period, the mark of a true guerrilla leader. During the siege Cronje fell ill, giving Koos a brief opportunity to experience leadership.

He later participated in the capture of the Jameson Raiders in January 1896, who had failed to instigate an uprising of British expatriate workers, known as Uitlanders, mostly because of the quick response of the Transvaal militia led by Piet Cronje.

The Lion of the Western Transvaal came to prominent attention in 1899 at the start of the Second Anglo-Boer War, when he was appointed a field general by Cronje who sent him to join the siege of Kimberley. Cronje's tactics were the diametric opposite of those favoured by Koos, namely, sieges and traditional fixed battles. This appointment led to the first confrontation of the war when Koos attacked an armoured train at Kraaipan, north of Kimberley on 12 October 1899.

This was a classic ambush. The Boer force arrived at the place of attack before the enemy and made all the necessary preparations, including the destruction of rails to force a derailment and the cutting of the telegraph wires to prevent effective reinforcement. The train, *The Mosquito*, was carrying two artillery pieces and the British commander continued towards the ambush despite several warnings, the hubris of a well-armed occupying force. The waiting Boers were warned when the locomotive ran off the rails and instead of reversing the armoured train, the British force attempted to repair it, accompanied by the train whistle blowing.

Koos de la Rey's force then attacked the British from both sides of the rails in the late night and exchanged gunfire until the arrival of the Boer artillery, which destroyed the locomotive boiler. This precipitated the surrender of the British force when the Boers seized the artillery pieces, rifles and ammunition. It was a classic guerrilla operation in familiar territory facing an over-confident government force in the dead of night with little chance of retreat from the attack. While this may have been a shot in the dark, it was more likely a specific intelligence-driven operation by a local insurgent force well informed by their urban and rural supporters.

This resounding, though small victory, drew support and confidence for Koos as a military leader, which led to him to taking on an increasing role in the Boer military hierarchy.

The victory at Kraaipan was followed by reversals at Belmont and Graspan the following November when the Boer tactic of hill or kopje positions exposed them to superior British artillery and frontal charges resulting in their urgent departure on horseback. A few days later De la Rey decided to change his tactics and prepared entrenched positions across the Modder River near a railway bridge destroyed by the Boers.

This tactic of deploying soldiers in trenches on flat ground reduced the effectiveness of the British artillery, while limiting casualties of a rebel army unlikely to see reinforcements or resupply. The British commander came on to what was in effect a prepared ambush, and lumbered into battle in a manner typical for a large force at the time. Koos de la Rey had lured the British into a bridge choke point not unlike Wallace's at Stirling or Bolivar's at Boyaca, and with equal results. The foreign invaders in unfamiliar territory, with no local contacts and surrounded by rebel supporters, had little or no intelligence and the minds of their commanders were skewed by overconfidence.

Lord Methuen, the British commander, began to feel the drain of soldiers and morale in the oppressive heat while pinned down in the open under constant and accurate Boer rifle fire, which was relieved only by the arrival of additional artillery. The opposing forces were equally matched in numbers and Boer casualties amounted to half the British losses in what petered out into a stalemate by nightfall. The Boer army then quietly left the battlefield unbeknownst to the British who rained artillery on empty trenches the next morning.

One British account refers to Modder Bridge as a successful action by Lord Methuen but nothing could be further from the truth. A professional army, centuries in the making, manned by experienced officers, wilted in the South African sun against an irregular but capable force led by a man of little experience and military education. The casualty lists and casual departure of the Boer force confirm this.

Koos was wounded at the Modder River and his son Adriaan was tragically killed. In an armed insurgency, nothing displays commitment and enhances morale as guerrilla leaders joined in the conflict by close family and friends who are sufficiently close to the action to incur casualties. It is a hard but effective reality that would escape a government or professional army, whose patriotism would run aground on the dedication of rebels loaded with emotional stamina from the loss of loved ones. The extended hostilities in Iraq and Syria are an example of fighters with extended family, tribal and religious connections remaining in the field of battle for years in the face of overwhelming odds, while tying down a national army with significant outside support in urban warfare.

Lord Methuen continued his advance along the railway line to relieve the siege of Kimberley, having been delayed several times by the actions of the Boer rebel forces led by Koos de la Rey. This tactic slowed the main opposing column, forcing casualties and depletion of resources while those under siege feared they might not be rescued. Koos then set up another attack at Magersfontein about twenty-five miles from the British target of Kimberley. At Magersfontein the railway passed to the west of a flat open area surrounded by hills that provided cover and a superior battlefield view for the assembled Boer force. The British were belatedly forced to deploy a balloon to try to grasp the lay of the land and ultimately, their perilous situation.

Like Bolivar's British Legion, the Boers had foreign volunteers in the shape of a Scandinavian Volunteer Corps numbering fewer than a hundred. However their small number belied their great bravery when the unit was decimated while holding their position at Magersfontein.

In previous encounters, superior British artillery firepower had forced Boer casualties and retreat. After several disputes with the military and political leadership, Koos was able to implement his plan of placing Boer troops in a long trench along the base of the hills to protect them from exposure to artillery shells and also deceive the British commander – their location in prior battles had been on the slopes of hills.

In a version of burning ships on arrival on foreign shores, as conquistador Hernan Cortes did on arrival in Mexico to ensure there could be no retreat, the Boers had no avenue of retreat – they would be forced to face the withering fire of British forces on the exposed slopes if they retreated from their trenches. One might suggest that the recent death and burial of his son Adriaan had hardened the general, the result being this tough almost fatalistic tactic.

The barely visible trenches were also protected by thick scrub brush and some wire fencing which would warn, expose and then trap any British frontal assaults. British attempts to scout the Boer positions were unsuccessful due to the terrain, farm fences and harassing fire from the Boers, who were natural sharpshooters. The Boer force had recently been armed with new Mauser rifles using smokeless ammunition giving them an increased effectiveness – the British had previously had superiority in battlefield equipment.

The presence of local workers within the British caravan, many of who supplied the Boers with intelligence, had forced Lord Methuen to limit knowledge of his battle plans within his force, which eventually led to some confusion by lower ranks in the ensuing battle. His plan was the classic British strategy – approach the likely battle site under cover of darkness and attack at dawn. The ramification of a column in alien territory surrounded by locals in support of a rebel force occurred many times in Vietnam, Afghanistan and Iraq.

On the afternoon of 10 December 1899, the British forces moved up towards the most southerly hill, Magersfontein Kop, under an artillery bombardment that failed to affect the Boers who were waiting at the base of the hill. Their field commander was Major General Wauchope, who had been ordered to keep his soldiers in a close-quarter column that provided deep and narrow targets for the able Boer marksmen the next day. He is said to have commented that this close formation was madness. The Boer force was approximately eight thousand men, and it was facing a British force of soldiers, cavalry and artillery, that totalled twice that number.

As a belated order came for an extended formation, the attacking British Army became noisily entangled in the Boer wire fence. At that point the Boers opened up with deadly accurate volleys, causing hundreds of casualties among the bunched-up British troops in the first few minutes of the battle.

Some British fled, some stayed and some attempted an advance to no avail. The attack petered out and many soldiers lay flat, seeking any cover, under harassing Boer fire as daylight froze them into inaction. Artillery was brought closer to the Boer position but extended fire had little impact over several hours. In the late afternoon, Boer artillery opened up on the cavalry. This was the straw that broke the camel's back and the sunburned British soldiers withdrew after Lord Methuen ordered a general retreat to their Modder River encampment.

It was a significant victory for a smaller, less equipped guerrilla army, that had forced battle at a certain place and in a manner of their choice. British casualties ran to almost a thousand while the Boers suffered less than a quarter of that number. The British commander Wauchope was killed, one of many officers and senior ranks. This was a demoralising blow that not only saw the British retreat, but led to a failure to relieve the siege of Kimberley.

Just the day before Magersfontein, the British had been mightily defeated at the battle of Stormberg, where hundreds of British soldiers were killed and captured. Later that week those two disasters were followed by a further defeat at Colenso, where even greater casualties and prisoners were inflicted by a third Boer guerrilla force. This period later became known as the Black Week.

One source confirmed de la Rey as the architect of the victory of Magersfontein but that he was absent on the actual day of combat, having gone off to inspect the state of forces besieging Kimberley. He was reportedly quite unhappy at the failure of the Boer field commanders to capitalise on the British retreat by undertaking a standard guerrilla tactic of harassing the rearguard of a retreating enemy.

This was also part of a larger failure in that the Boer guerrillas, from the different nascent republics, chose not to expand their attacks on the British, thereby passing up the chance to capitalise on their successes by attempting a military coup de grace and instead allowing the British to reconstitute its army into a larger, updated, well-armed force. The end result was that the following year saw entire Boer armies surrender and their political leadership in exile. Part of the reason for this was a dogged insistence to maintain a domestic independence stance for each republic instead of a wider national liberation movement, which was the end result in any event when the country separated from the British many years later.

General Koos de la Rey neither surrendered nor went into the safety of exile, but joined like-minded Boer commanders in an extensive guerrilla war mostly in the Western Transvaal with his commando or militia. It was a difficult time to be in the field as the British pursued an aggressive policy of attrition by burning farms and incarcerating Boer families in concentration camps where tens of thousands of children, women and the elderly died of starvation and disease. It required a hard guerrilla heart to continue the struggle but the British actions – which would be considered war crimes today – gave much impetus to a core cadre of several thousand mounted guerrillas.

Koos and the Boer guerrilla army proceeded to force a succession of victories, at Moedwil, Nooitgedacht, Driefontein, Donkerhoek or Diamond Hill, on a British army that was struggling to maintain effective control over a vast country. The British were forced to thinly disperse their troops, and these smaller groups were often subject to attacks by a larger Boer column. British casualties at these battles numbered in the many hundreds but on at least one occasion the Boers faced an army three times their number at Donkerhoek. The general conducted a series of attacks on weakly defended British outposts and transportation hubs culminating in February 1902 when Uncle Koos ambushed a British column from Wolmaranstad at the Ysterspruit River, south-west of Johannesburg, that reaped huge quantities of ammunition and supplies badly needed by the transient guerrilla force with no logistical support.

Lord Methuen then decided to lead a punitive expedition to retaliate and capture General de la Rey. The majority of his troops were inexperienced, as the extended warfare had the British Empire scraping the bottom of the barrel in order to try to keep a lid on an extended native insurgency. Things did not go as planned. On 7 March 1902 de La Rey and his men, many wearing khaki that would have confused British onlookers, conducted a mounted attack on Methuen's column, likely at several points to immediately divide the enemy and spread panic. The cavalry fled whereupon the guerrillas surrounded the wagons before raining fire on the remaining foot soldiers. Lord Methuen was shot and his horse fell on him, resulting in a broken leg. Even a doctor approaching Methuen was shot. Failing any escape, with several hundred dead, wounded and captured, Lord Methuen surrendered.

The lightning strike, the divided column and a ferocious hail of fire from a roadside bush line constituted a classic guerrilla ambush that rewarded a parochial independence movement with one of the greatest victories of all time against the British Empire.

General Jacobus 'Koos' de la Rey. (Anglo-Boer War Museum)

In contrast to some modern guerrilla conflicts, where the captured and wounded could have expected execution or years as hostages (but normal for the Victorian era), General De la Rey pragmatically and diplomatically, in a war ebbing towards a Boer defeat, released Methuen and his prisoners. The limited Boer supplies and guerrilla warfare did not allow for a prisoner-of-war camp in any event.

Although he had achieved a great shock defeat of the British, with many artillery pieces captured, Koos came in for much criticism for Methuen's release. In the end this became a moot point as there was a general Boer surrender the following May. Koos had performed admirably under difficult circumstances, leaving the field of battle with his reputation and integrity intact. After the surrender, General de la Rey went on to fundraise abroad for war orphans and widows as well as to seek the return of interned Boer soldiers to their homeland. Later elected to the Transvaal parliament, he participated in the creation of what became the Union of South Africa in 1910 that included the Boer republics.

Being a man of the bible, Koos likely relied on the urging of the Ecclesiastes verse: 'a time for war, and a time for peace'.

The outbreak of World War I with Germany – who had supported the Boer struggle – saw a conflicted Koos de la Rey sit back, while quietly opposing Boer participation against their former friend alongside their former oppressors. On 15 September 1914, he was shot in the back at a police roadblock while travelling on official business and thereby a persistent, successful thorn of oppression, a leader in waiting for any potential uprising during the war with Germany, was eliminated.

He was not to be afforded the same Victorian courtesy of a quiet old age with his family, that he had extended to hundreds on the battlefield.

CHAPTER 5

KING ABDULAZIZ BIN ABDUL RAHMAN AL SAUD, SAUDI ARABIA

The modern Saudi Arabia did not exist at the turn of the 20th century. It was the creation of the remarkable King Abdulaziz Bin Abdul Rahman Al Saud, believed to have been born between 1875 and 1880. Like many guerrilla leaders, he endured oppression and hardship in his youth when his family, then resident in what is modern day Riyadh, had to flee from a rival tribe called the Rashidis. At the time, Riyadh was in a small, sparsely populated and desolate part of the Middle East known as the Nejd which, along with other nearby areas, was ruled by different tribes. The Emirate of Nejd is regarded as the second Saudi state, having evolved from the earlier Emirate of Ad-Dar'iyah which existed from the 18th century until destruction in a war with the Ottoman-supported Egyptian, Ibrahim Pasha, in 1818. Abdullah bin Saud, then ruler of the Al Saud tribe was taken to Istanbul by the Ottomans, where he was executed. The second Saudi state, the Emirate of Nejd, fared no better when the Rashidis defeated the Al Saud alliance in 1891 at the battle of al-Mulayda, forcing the Al Saud family into exile with several neighbouring states, but finally in Kuwait for a decade.

One account states that prior to taking up residence in Kuwait, Al Saud, then a youth, spent a significant amount of time with the Al Murrah Bedouin tribe learning the traits of the Bedouin which would have included desert navigation, finding an oasis and travelling long distances by camel. Like George Washington or Koos de la Rey, these early life experiences proved immensely valuable in later conflict.

Although exiled and poor in Kuwait, the young Al Saud was able to take the first of his several wives. He went on to have a large family of forty-three sons and fifty daughters. A large family at the time provided the clan leader not only with warriors for any potential conflict but daughters to secure alliances. At that time, what is now Saudi Arabia was fragmented into different regions among many tribes, some with outside support and contact either with the British or the Ottomans of Turkey.

As with any region with multiple areas and leaders, conflict for territorial acquisition or raids for profit were a regular part of life, which Al Saud took advantage of in 1901. He was not yet thirty and he led a force of fewer than fifty men. His objective was to recapture the family seat of Riyadh but the road to Riyadh was circuitous. Along the way Al Saud was able to grow his small army before disappearing into the large desert area known as The Empty Quarter or Rub' al Khali. This act would confuse his enemies into thinking that he had vanished or returned to Kuwait – disinformation in its most basic form.

Any force of soldiers in a fixed position, such as a fort, will lose their operational effectiveness over time especially where there are repeated unfulfilled threats of attack over several months. Such was the position of the Rashidi governor of Riyadh, then resident in the Masmak fortress or citadel when the leader of the rival Al Saud clan attacked with fewer than a hundred warriors. Although Al Saud's gathered force was initially much larger, fear of Ottoman or Rashidi reprisal caused many to desert prior to the eventual attack.

Al Saud and his small band spent several weeks at the Yabrin oasis in the Rub' al Khali awaiting the end of the Muslim religious holiday, Ramadan, which that year was 10 January 1902, before he raided the fort. In this he followed the well-worn – but likely unknown to him – steps of George Washington, who attacked Trenton on Christmas Eve or Bolivar, who attacked Cucuta during Lent.

Al Saud approached the fortress under the cover of darkness, to await dawn when he proposed to attack the fort as that was when the gates first opened for the day. Prior to departure he left a message

Masmak Fort, Riyadh, Saudi Arabia, 2014. (Francisco Anzola/Wikmedia Commons)

with a few supporters, telling them that they were to wait a day to hear of success or to carry news of his death and the attacking force to their families. Such a declaration would have emboldened his force – not unlike George Washington putting the frozen Trenton River to the back of his troops or Koos de la Rey putting the back of his forces to an open kopje at Magersfontein.

In the early morning light, as the Rashidi governor emerged from the safety of his fortress, Al Saud attacked. The small group tried to retreat but failed and the raiders entered the Masmak Fort, killing many of its defenders and the governor in the ensuing skirmish.

Al Saud had spent some time in preparation for the attack, from gathering warriors, to close oversight the night before the early morning attack. Such preparation over an extended period and timing, although for a relatively small but well defended target, has become a regular tactic even today, with FARC cadres carefully monitoring a small police station in a rural town and making plans before attempting to seize it.

This small victory, many years in the making, propelled Al Saud into the popular consciousness and made his small defeat of the ruling Rashidis a great propaganda event as word spread through what was to be, his future kingdom. Like Washington at Trenton, and Bolivar at Boyaca, this victory seemed to pave the road to a new nation and potential followers began to flock to his cause while ignoring petty rivalries or old tribal feuds.

Shortly thereafter Al Saud was installed as the Saudi leader in the Great Mosque of Riyadh by his father, with many prominent citizens present to see him receive the Saud sword of leadership under the name for which he was most known, Ibn Saud. All subsequent kings of Saudi Arabia included the name Ibn Saud. He was also referred to as King Abdulaziz.

The renewed Saud–Rashidi conflict drew interest from the outside world with Germany supporting the Rashidis and Britain starting a very long association with the House of Saud. Like many of his guerrilla predecessors – Washington with the French and Koos de la Rey with the Germans – Ibn Saud wisely made the enemy of his enemies, his friend.

The Rashidis, who were from Ha'il in what is north-west Saudi Arabia today, initially avoided further direct conflict with Riyadh, which allowed Ibn Saud to consolidate his gains while expanding his influence and forces. Those who failed to rally to Ibn Saud were attacked and in a relatively short time he was able to expand his area of control while dissipating any attempted concentration of Rashidi forces.

That summer of 1902 the Rashidi leader conducted a series of raids but failed to capture a now heavily fortified Riyadh while facing hostility from a number of tribes allied to Ibn Saud. The Rashidis became invaders of an area they had previously occupied and like all invaders, they became subject to attack from every direction, their every movement monitored. Indiscipline and opportunistic raids by some of the Rashidi forces as they followed Ibn Saud south of Riyadh, dissipated command and control, which gave Ibn Saud the initiative, as he drew the Rashidis further from their home base. This culminated in a battle between several thousand tribal warriors at Dilam in November 1902 when Ibn Saud surprised them with extensive rifle fire before a cavalry charge that saw several hundred Rashidi casualties before they fled.

It was Ibn Saud's second consecutive and much greater military victory facing a larger, well-equipped force, who were far from home, in a climate of local uprising. Although not a foreign incursion by any means, it might as well have been, as the Rashidis began to face what the British had felt in 1297 Scotland,1776 America and 1899 South Africa. This is a lesson proved across centuries of guerrilla warfare from 13th-century Scotland to 21st-century Mosul, that invaders both foreign or local interests who become oppressive can expect eventual expulsion however long an armed struggle this will require.

Thereafter Ibn Saud was faced with a series of failed attacks by the Rashidis culminating in a joint expedition with the Turks in 1904. The Ottoman empire had almost exclusive influence over this area for a very long time and faced with the rising power of Ibn Saud they decided to send an expedition from modern-day Iraq of several thousand Turkish soldiers into the Nejd to retain their historic control. Unwisely, the Ottoman Rashidi force entered their target region in the extreme heat of summer. They were subject to marauding attacks by the Saud forces and by October there were only a few hundred left, with sickness and desertion playing a major part in this attrition.

In his response to the Ottoman invasion, Ibn Saud displayed true guerrilla leadership qualities, by allowing an invading force to enter an inhospitable environment surrounded by hostile and mobile forces for a campaign in which set battles would play no part, allowing the environment and occasional ambush to blunt the offensive. There was another attempt to fight Ibn Saud in 1905 which was dissipated by an uprising in Yemen that forced the Turks to minimise their troop allocation to the leader of the Rashidi clan, Ibn Rashid, who was subsequently killed in 1906.

The failed Turkish intrusions as well as the decline of the Rashidi clan allowed Ibn Saud to consolidate his hold on the Nejd region when the Turks withdrew following a treaty he agreed with them in 1906, whereby he pretended to recognise the authority of the Ottomans. His repeated attempts after that to engage British support produced no concrete results as they were wary of Ottoman displeasure until it suited their interest with the onset of World War I, nearly a decade later.

Ibn Saud had, through a mastery of diplomacy, alliances and military acumen, reinstated the House of Saud in the Nejd but did not inherit a wealthy kingdom. His nascent nation was one of the most sparsely populated and poorest areas of the world with few resources and no outside aid from foreign countries. The rush to be a friend of the future state of Saudi Arabia would await the discovery of oil, but in the interim he had to maneuver his way past the dominating powers in the Middle East of the Ottoman empire and Britain to grow his proposed country.

For several years after, Ibn Saud had to endure the occasional attacks by the Ottoman puppet, Sharif Hussein, as well as being banned from the holy cities of Mecca and Medina. As an experienced guerrilla leader, Ibn Saud leaned away when confronted by superior forces, recognising that a war with the Ottoman proxies would have to wait until his logistical and political position improved. This did not stop Ibn Saud from stirring up hostility in the eastern region of Al-Ahsa, largely ignored by the Ottomans, in preparation for a complete takeover of the area in 1913.

The classic guerrilla strategy of provoking local unrest before an attempt to bring a neighbouring area under control would provide a morale boost by expansion of territory, a buffer zone against opponents and another potential haven in any future conflict. A modern example of this would be the FARC guerrillas of Colombia operating from the Arauca province on the border with Venezuela where they could find safe bases when pressured by the Colombian army.

Shortly before his conquest in Al-Ahsa, Ibn Saud helped to create the Ikhwan or brotherhood, a religious militia based on belief in a branch of the Sunni Muslim faith known as Wahhabism. This ferocious band of fighters became the tip of his spear as he expanded his domain, with the support of irregular forces from different tribes in all directions. A variation of this exists even today in Iraq where the government forces are being supported by the Shia, Popular Mobilisation Units.

Rarely in a guerrilla struggle does a major international power approach a rebel group to make a political and territorial treaty, but this was exactly what happened when the British government

The history of **counter-insurgency** or anti-guerrilla methodology has almost always seen government forces allied with local militia, usually recruited from a different ethnic group, religious persuasion or geographical region within a country. A guerrilla movement based on a particular ideology, such as the FARC in Colombia, face a much harder path than a country deeply divided by religious faiths. This situation has presented itself in places such as Northern Ireland, Syria and Iraq where religious beliefs are associated with particular geographical areas. Put another way, governments, oppressors or invaders have a larger chance of containing rebel groups or achieving eventual success in a country with a singular religion than one divided by large swathes of different religious groups. Proof positive was the recent FARC peace treaty after decades of inconclusive insurgency.

recognised Ibn Saud's claim to lands in what was to become Saudi Arabia, whilst providing military support in the 1915 Treaty of Darin. Ibn Saud was in his ascendancy and the British, fighting a war against Germany and the Turks, wisely sought him out. The disaster of the Turkish victory at Gallipoli was to provide a hindsight endorsement of this small but important diplomatic initiative. From a mere refugee in Kuwait, Ibn Saud now had the support of an important international ally and resources to deal a death blow to the triple scourges of the House of Saud: the Turks, their Rashidi allies and Sherif Hussein of the holy city of Mecca, now also a British ally against the Ottoman empire.

Ibn Saud was forced to keep a low profile in his feud with the Sherif of Mecca during World War I, but it was open season on the Rashidis who were in a perpetual state of decline. In 1921, Ibn Saud attacked the Rashidi stronghold of Ha'il, several hundred miles north of Riyadh in a pincer move from the south joined by an attack from the north by the allied Rwala tribe. The Rashidi emirate collapsed some two decades after, forcing the Al Saud family into exile and they became the virtual prisoners of the House of Saud before completely disappearing as a political force in that region.

Mecca, 1907. (T. E. Lawrence/Wikimedia Commons)

The success of Ibn Saud substantially expanded his territory, sufficiently so, that a second treaty was signed with the British in 1922 at Uqair on the eastern coast. It might seem incredible today that a guerrilla army would seize areas by force and have their gains recognised not once, but twice, by a premier world power. This was not a uniform expanse of land and people but a series of small regional emirates, a federation before unification. In this, Ibn Saud proved that diplomatic skills were as important as military ability, a lesson learned too late by other guerrilla leaders, including Jonas Savimbi and Velupillai Prabhakaran.

Ibn Saud then turned his attention to the last barrier to his new nation, the Hashemite kingdom, including the holy enclaves of Mecca and Medina, which he proceeded to capture in 1924 and 1926 respectively.

The elite of the Ibn Saud guerrilla force was his conservative Ikhwan militia, who were in effect a permanent camel cavalry that enabled him to launch military excursions without complete reliance on allied tribal warriors. The Ikhwan had always looked down on any alliance with the British *kuffar* or infidels, and they began to stir up rebellion after the conquest of Mecca and Medina, as the prospect of a new country began to take on a greater reality.

*Ikhwan militia, 1916. (*Al-Musawar *magazine 1954/Wikimedia Commons)*

It is not an unknown paradox that guerrilla struggles on the cusp of victory, and even thereafter, become subject to internecine disputes and rivalries followed by the disappearance of leadership rivals. Such was the fate of many in the Chinese, Cuban and Nicaraguan revolutions. In Nicaragua, a daring commander like Eden Pastora, who rescued leadership from prison and captured the public imagination, incurred the enmity of an insecure cartel of leadership, causing him to be sidelined and eventually constructively exiled.

The Ikhwan commanders, who had done much of the heavy lifting to secure the future state of Saudi Arabia, began to see themselves as the power behind the nation and not merely inhabitants of that region. Despite being banned by Ibn Saud, the Ikhwan continued raiding neighbouring communities that were under British protection following the treaty with Ibn Saud. After a Sharia court had ruled against the Ishwan – which they ignored – Ibn Saud then attempted to negotiate with the commander of the Ikhwan forces to resolve the matter peaceably, but it was not to be.

The Ikhwan commander was brimming with overconfidence and felt that he could crush the Ibn Saud forces, who he regarded as mere town folk and not fundamentalist Bedouin warriors. Ibn Saud began to make preparations for battle, including traditional payments to tribal chiefs and their warriors. He relied on his two brothers and sons as commanders in the field to provide a strong backbone for the attack. History has many instances of family members supporting a guerrilla leader in a conflict such as Fidel Castro's brother, who was at his side throughout the Cuban Revolution and later became president. Koos de la Rey lost a son on the field of battle at the Modder River in 1899.

On 30 March 1929, Ibn Saud led his forces against the Ikhwan at Sibilla where the British-supplied truck-mounted machine guns decimated the Ikhwan on their camels in the open desert. By one estimate the Ikhwan lost a thousand men to a few hundred Ibn Saud losses. Later that year Ibn Saud organised an audacious surprise night attack on the Ikhwan remnants at Hafr Al-Batin in the north-east, near the Iraqi border.

Rather than allow an opposing and dissident group, formerly part of a guerrilla column, to seek safe haven and continue opposition, Ibn Saud sought to completely eliminate what he perceived to be a threat to the struggle for a new country. Simon Bolivar and Chairman Mao did not seek open battle with any naysayers, but simply had them executed.

The Ikhwan leader, seriously wounded at Sibilla, eventually surrendered to the British in January 1930 and the Ikhwan militia was completely disbanded with many leaders imprisoned. With the elimination of the only serious opposition to the supremacy of Ibn Saud, many tribes beat a path to his door, to join not only an obvious success story but the major local military power in the region.

This did not completely stop future revolts within the Ibn Saud domain, but he fended them all off in a most ruthless and consistent manner. The outcome of a localised dispute with Ibn Saud was certain – he completely destroyed all rebel opposition to his reign in every scenario and such groups could rely on Ibn Saud having a single response, death to all.

In 1932, Ibn Saud suppressed an uprising in Hejaz with his cavalry and British-supplied armoured cars, killing hundreds of rebels, followed by the beheading of their leader and public display of his head. Such ferocity was a trademark of Ibn Saud and the boundaries of his territory grew. In most cases guerrilla leaders will

Ibn Saud and Franklin D. Roosevelt, 1945. (U.S. Navy Naval History and Heritage Command/Wikimedia Commons)

always attempt to kill rivals. It was a necessary evil for a guerrilla leader seeking to unite his people under a common banner before the transition to a legitimate and recognised state. In this he was no different to Mao Zedong and Simon Bolivar.

On 23 September 1932, Ibn Saud declared the Kingdom of Saudi Arabia and proceeded to initially rule from the genesis of his many accomplishments, the Masmak Fort in Riyadh, before the completion of his Murabba Palace in 1938.

The discovery of oil in the region, particularly in Bahrain, led to exploration and the discovery of oil in Saudi Arabia in 1936 followed by the start of production in 1938. The discovery was made in the barren Al-Ahsa region which had been acquired by Ibn Saud in 1913, being largely ignored by the Rashidis and Turks. It provided a foundation for a future of great prosperity for Saudi Arabia.

Guerrilla leaders often arise in countries where there are significant natural resources which are being exploited by the few, such as in Angola, South Africa and Colombia. It is a natural school of thought that their struggle and the resistance thereto, cannot only be about equal distribution and social justice but self-enrichment.

To his great and everlasting credit, Ibn Saud was a purist guerrilla leader who relentlessly pursued the unification of his vision of a nation to lift his countrymen out of poverty and backwardness into the modern world. It will be left to those who follow him to creep their way forward in a region full of conflict, more recently, with the Houthis of Yemen.

CHAPTER 6

MAO ZEDONG, CHINA

Mao Zedong, later known as Chairman Mao, was born just before the turn of the 20th century to a prosperous farming family in Hunan province, southern China. Like many guerrilla leaders who did not come from poverty, including Washington and Bolivar, his background afforded him the opportunity for education that provided a firm base for an open and far-reaching mind, much needed for the struggles that lay ahead of him.

Mao had a significant amount of schooling, as well as access to a diverse range of books. These contributed to his political consciousness of the pressing needs of equality for the poor in a stratified and divided country, desperately in need of unification. In this belief, two polar opposites of ideology, King Ibn Saud and Mao were conjoined.

Although predominantly a rural and peasant-dominated society, early 20th-century China had seen its share of social uprisings and revolutions, one of the last few being the Xinhai Revolution in 1911, which saw the end of Chinese imperial dynasties and the creation of the Republic of China. Mao was old enough to support this revolution, which provided an opportunity for him to observe first-hand the popular discontent, the organisation of people, the leadership and eventually the success of the revolution. The leader of that revolution, Sun Yat-Sen, also first president of China, made an indelible impression on the young Mao who

Many earlier guerrilla leaders came to their struggle not by book learning or political education but the desperation of their immediate reality, for example Scotsman William Wallace or Manuel Marulanda of the Colombian FARC. Such a **miserable daily existence** reveals the common denominators of any guerrilla struggle for centuries: poverty, unequal distribution of land, lack of basic services and access to education, concentration of wealth and power in the hands of a select few due to ethnicity, tribal affiliation or simple effluxion of time.

These factors reveal a template that predicted the present conflicts in the Middle East and will repeat itself many times in the future. A persistent failure of colonial authorities to develop their territories before and after departure, a succession of military dictatorships, a continuum of tribal- or religious-based leaderships, all guarantee future guerrilla struggles that will be like global trade, on an international scale.

The most likely remedy lies in a developed world sufficiently committed to the Third World countries that historically provided human and mineral resources for the development of leading countries today, now forced to commit larger budgets for border protection, anti-terrorism and a seemingly unending cycle of aid for famines. Proof positive lies in the unending stream of refugees, internal culture conflicts and urban attacks that unfortunately reveal the new world paradigm.

referred to Sun frequently in his writings on the foundation of modern China.

Mao went on to apply to several entities as he searched for direction including soap makers, a police academy and several schools before ending up at a business school. This pleased his father, but being taught in English, he was forced to abandon that plan. In the path of many an autodidact, Mao started visiting the local library in Changsa, the capital of Hunan province, from opening to closing every day. He went on to attend the First Normal School of Hunan until 1918 while maintaining an almost religious dedication to reading newspapers and material about world geography.

Mao Zedong, 1913. (Wikimedia Commons)

World War I saw Japan invade Shandong province to lay siege to the German-controlled city of Tsingtaoi as well as imposing certain restrictions on China. During this time of international flux, Mao's fellow students began to gather around him for weekly reports on world affairs as he was able to explain them in a comprehensive and understandable manner. He was a keen listener to other points of view, which he would later dissect in reply. This singular characteristic not only helped to develop his leadership skills but sharpened a keen mind to assess unfolding world events that related to China as he beat a path for a modern and independent China.

Mao eventually ended up at university in Peking during a period of regular protests against Japanese intervention and corruption in government. He later returned to Hunan province and like Bolivar with the *Correo del Orinoco*, began publication of the *Xiang River Review* in 1919, using the paper to speak out for unity and against oppression. Contrary to popular belief, he did not establish the Communist Party in China in 1921, but was one of the several founders that led him to become party secretary in Hunan Province.

Political developments and the death of Sun Yat-Sen resulted in the ascension of Chiang Kai-shek, leader of a rival nationalist

World knowledge and up-to-date news were, and are, essential components for a successful guerrilla leader to plot a course of least resistance for the struggle and maximum gains for international support. These tenets were noticeably followed by Washington, Bolivar, Savimbi and the various FARC leaders. The debris following successful air strikes on FARC commanders invariably included small radios, used to monitor news, among other equally important possessions such as rifles and ammunition. Most guerrilla struggles would see some members of the leadership posted abroad to maintain relations with friendly nations as well as keep the leadership informed of developments on the world stage. An example of this was Pedro 'Tito' Chingunji, the Foreign Secretary for the UNITA of Angola, who was a well-liked and effective communicator for the UNITA cause abroad. Unfortunately for Tito, Savimbi – like many guerrilla leaders who embraced a policy of seeing off any rivals – had him killed.

group called the Kuomintang or KMT, to become the titular leader of China. In 1927 Chiang Kai-shek attacked the Communists in their powerbase of Shanghai. Prior to this Mao had been an established Communist party leader, advocating – like Bolivar and his declaration of death – that the struggle required execution of their opponents, mainly landlords at that time. Chiang and the KMT took him at his word and began a wholesale slaughter of members of the Communist party in Shanghai. The Communists responded with an armed uprising of some militia under their control in Nanchang as well as several peasant uprisings elsewhere, which marked the start of the civil war with the KMT.

After some skirmishes, they followed a common feature of guerrilla warfare – the strategy of retreat to rural provinces such as Fujian to the south, where they enjoyed the support of their peasant base who provided food and intelligence support while neutralising the KMT with a simple tactic – distance. Before the retreat, Mao additionally pursued a ruthless course of elimination and subjugation of political and military rivals in a Chinese Communist Party substantially controlled and funded by the Soviets. He regularly purged the peasants and other non-CCP members who opposed or criticised him, all of which was accomplished with the tacit approval of the Russian overlords.

By 1929, Mao was in control of the Red Army, the military wing of the Chinese Communist Party that was designed to impose their ideology on the Chinese by force if necessary and to fight the KMT. His rise had involved the execution of nearly ten thousand of its soldiers to stifle dissent and precipitate the rise of a man with no military training or experience who had a known proclivity for the luxuries of life. He had accumulated a large staff to meet his every need and an ever-expanding contingent of bodyguards to ensure his safety. Travelling frequently between several seized luxury houses, he would always have an escape route prepared.

In December 1930, although facing several rebel uprisings that reduced available troops, the KMT sent an expedition of under ten thousand to the isolated mountains of Jiangxi against the new leader of the Red Army numbering forty thousand with civilian support. The KMT was deprived of any local resources which limited the range of re-supply and thereby, its operational area. In this, Mao turned every citizen under his control into an irregular soldier who was required to demolish anything of use to the invading KMT while denying them access to people and information.

Early one morning, in mountains immersed in fog, Mao sprang his ambush on the KMT troops acting as forward scouts while observing the action from a distance. By afternoon, Mao was victorious in his first military victory, a victory that saw almost the entire KMT force captured and their commander beheaded with his head sent down the river as a warning to any future expedition. Mao was also rewarded with arms and most importantly, radios and their operators. This first early victory, like that of Washington and Ibn Saud, became a lasting springboard for future success and the journey to create a new state, though not without pitfalls along the way.

Undeterred, the KMT organised a second punitive expedition in April 1931, but were again defeated by Mao's tactics of distance, sparsity of local supplies and ensuring there were no locals from whom to extract intelligence. Mao was assisted in that encounter by Russian-supplied radio-interception equipment, which aided the anticipation of enemy movements – enabling repeated ambushes.

Incensed by the losses of the two expeditions, in July 1931 Chiang Kai-shek, commanded a force of several hundred thousand men into the Red Army area and unlike previous incursions, they maintained occupation of the area abandoned by Mao. This meant that Mao was temporarily unable to return, use his intelligence advantage or conduct effective ambushes to weaken the opposing force.

Sometimes a guerrilla leader is saved by intelligence, the failure of his opponents or the intervention of an event or foreign force that tips the balance in a war. For George Washington, this was the French intervention in the American Revolution, for Simon Bolivar it was the reluctance of Spain to commit more resources to the South American wars of independence, for General Vo Nguyen Giap it was the defeat of the French at Dien Bien Phu.

As the KMT nationalist force expanded control over China, elements within Japan felt threatened and in September 1931, the Japanese army invaded Manchuria in north-east China, an area that extended to the eastern coast facing Japan. This cataclysmic event in the history of China saw the KMT temporarily withdraw from conflict with the Red Army and by November 1931, Mao and the Chinese Communist Party had, somewhat prematurely, proclaimed a new state although they were still a provincial guerrilla force facing a much larger and better-equipped internal rival, as well as a foreign invader.

The KMT subsequently began a series of encirclement campaigns to contain any expansion of Mao's territory, blockade any reinforcement, recruitment or re-supply combined with periodic bombing of suspected leadership hideouts. After making a truce with the Japanese, in September 1933 the KMT constructed access roads with mini-forts in close proximity to each other for mutual protection not dissimilar to the strategy that would later be employed by the French in Indochina.

Supported by several hundred thousand troops, the KMT began to clear one area after another, reducing the operational area of the Red Army, while making the ever-reducing encirclement area easier to secure. This finally led to Mao Zedong and the remnants of his army, with the exception of a rearguard and decoy force, being forced to flee Jiangxi in October 1934 to begin what became known as the Long March – an exodus that eventually covered some 6,000 miles. This counter-guerrilla or counter-insurgency strategy was later deployed partially in Colombia over several decades against the FARC, which eventually led to successful peace talks in Cuba. A refinement of this initiative was the targeted killing of FARC leadership and innovative government campaigns that encouraged desertion of scare guerrilla troops which eventually saw the FARC leadership seeking to stop the conflict and trying to emerge as a political not a military force.

The Long March began with the political leadership, accompanied by Red Army units numbering about 80,000, breaking out in a western direction as that offered the least resistance, and indeed their passage was even allowed by some KMT blockhouses that had been so ordered or bribed, as the KMT leadership had apparently decided to allow the columns an initial avenue of escape. Desertion, disease and death caused a tremendous attrition and by December only half of the initial group crossed the Xiang River. The KMT then attacked those who had not crossed, decimating the rearguard. By attacking the rearguard without confronting the main column, Chiang and the KMT avoided large-scale direct confrontation but strengthened their presence in surrounding areas as they sought to direct the Long March towards Shaanxi province in central China. They viewed this strategy as an attempt to drive the Chinese warlords occupying areas in the path of the Long March into the open arms of the KMT and thereby extending the KMT-controlled territory. It would also present an opportunity for the Red Army to blunt any Japanese invasion.

Initially Mao and the Red Army travelled nearly a thousand miles west, to the province of Guizhou, where they encountered and defeated a local nationalist force at Liping before continuing on to Zunyi, which was captured in January 1935. At this point the KMT had not devoted any substantial resources towards the Red Army partially due to their diversion strategy and also due to extended supply lines, which prevented encirclement or blockhouses.

A guerrilla force of inferior size when confronted by a superior and better-equipped enemy will always **retreat**, but when the retreat becomes a march of thousands of miles over inhospitable territory with little government control, it is transformed into a deployment that sees new captured territory and local supply.

The Long March was not a continuous trek, but was broken up into travel to various destinations such as Guizou or Shaanxi in southern and northern China, as the Red Army manoeuvred to avoid the KMT in a circling motion that would have bewildered even the greatest military mind. This extended retreat lasted some three hundred and seventy days over every imaginable geographical feature including mountains, rivers and barren highlands. By this arduous route, Mao was able to preserve his forces not only by an extensive and continuous retreat, but by a journey through some of the most inhospitable territory in China.

This strategy was repeated in a more permanent way with the FARC of Colombia who operated from mountainous jungles in northern and southern Colombia, often with the borders of Venezuela and Ecuador to their back, which ensured avenues of retreat as the pursuing government army was hesitant to effect cross-border incursions. A similar theory was followed by Velupillai Prabhakaran of the LTTE during the civil war in Sri Lanka, which saw the LTTE operating from the Jaffna peninsula in the north with protection of the sea on three sides. During the Angolan civil war, Jonah Savimbi of UNITA operated from the barely accessible provinces of Moxico and Cuando Cubango in the south-east, near the border with Zambia, aptly described by the former Portuguese rulers as the land at the end of the earth.

The Long March was not undertaken by a single army column but several armies under different commanders moving in the same general direction. In 1935, near Zunyi in Guizhou province, Mao encountered the KMT, who attempted to encircle and destroy this particular Red Army column. There followed a number of

Rivers have provided a useful ally to guerrilla armies throughout the ages starting with William Wallace, who used the River Forth to provide a substantial barrier that forced the English through the choke point of Stirling Bridge and eventual defeat. Washington crossed the Delaware River in the dark during winter to exploit the false sense of security that this water barrier provided to the German allies of England. Bolivar crushed the Spanish at Boyaca Bridge over the Teatinos River, while Koos de la Rey used the Modder River as a neat foil to superior English numbers and artillery.

skirmishes between the two groups as Mao sought to evade the superior KMT army with the Red Army famously crossing the Chishui River four times before successfully fighting off the KMT at Loushan Pass.

Mao was not content to pursue a lengthy retreat through difficult territory, but followed an uneven course of circular, zig-zag and even reverse marches to confuse the KMT. He also made several feigned attacks on regional cities such as Kunming in the southern province of Yunnan, which caused panic and confusion among the KMT leadership who fled in the face of such seemingly close and unexpected attacks.

In May 1935, the Red Army was able to cross the Yangtze River, but the crossing took over a week due to the limited number of boats available. The boats were then burned to prevent further pursuit by the KMT but this was not the end of obstacles facing the Red Army as high mountains, supply shortages and local warlords would dog their journey north. At that time the various sections of the Red Army, sometimes described as the First, Second, Third and Fourth Armies began to slowly converge on their final destination, Shaanxi province in central China.

The Long March – six thousand miles over one year – equated to over sixteen miles a day which appears unbelievable at first glance but the likelihood was that only the main leadership column managed this pace as the rest of the various armies were

Chishui River. (Wikimedia Commons/Fanghong)

strung out across various regions and over numerous miles. These Red Army leaders had the benefit of a substantial number of assistants and porters who facilitated their travel by carrying them in two-man litters even over mountains, swamps and rice paddies.

The remote northern China enclave of the reunited Red Army allowed it to rebuild itself while strengthening its peasant base, which eventually propelled what was a fugitive guerrilla army into an eventual partner with the KMT in the war against the Japanese in 1937. Unlike the more classic KMT government army, guerrilla tactics and experience served the Red Army well in the fight against the Japanese, undertaken mostly behind enemy lines in the mountains.

One very useful feature of guerrilla operation among rural populations was the three rules of discipline and eight points of attention instituted by Mao among Red Army troops to ensure peasants were treated well and maintained their support. This was a far cry from the brutal treatment and executions performed by the Red Army in their earlier struggles and flight from the KMT. The difference perhaps was that once Mao decided on a permanent base in Shaanxi he recognised the need to maintain cordial relations and support of the locals.

The three rules of discipline, as listed in Graff and Higham's *A Military History of China*:

1. Obey orders in all your actions.
2. Do not take a single needle or piece of thread from the masses.
3. Turn in everything captured.

The eight points of attention:

1. Speak politely.
2. Pay fairly for what you buy.
3. Return everything you borrow.
4. Pay for anything you damage.
5. Do not hit or swear at people.
6. Do not damage crops.
7. Do not take liberties with women.
8. Do not ill-treat captives.

By the end of World War II, the Red Army had grown to over a million troops spread over an extensive area incorporating many provinces of northern China. In 1949 the remnants of a defeated KMT army fled to Taiwan and the People's Republic of China was proclaimed by Mao on 1 October.

The early ragtag Red Army eluded destruction while punishing the KMT with the attrition of distance and difficult geography. The lesson of this record goes back to Sun Tzu as an overarching principle of guerrilla warfare – avoid the strong and attack the weak.

CHAPTER 7

GENERAL VO NGUYEN GIAP, VIETNAM

The father, sister and wife of famed Vietnamese General Vo Nguyen Giap all died as a result of incarceration by the French colonial authorities during their administration of Vietnam. Their incarceration was part of a failed attempt to intimidate or punish the pro-nationalist Vietnamese, who were causing dissent among the population, that ran strong in the family. Many years later the general extracted a great military success and a settling of scores by the destruction of French forces at Dien Bien Phu in 1954 –revenge, a thousand fold. The result of that battle was over 13,000 French soldiers killed or dying in captivity.

Born shortly after the turn of the 20th century, Giap was – like many of his fellow guerrilla kings – a son of relative prosperity. His family was active in an anti-colonial insurgency against the French at the end of the 19th century called the Can Vuong Movement and his father was arrested for subversive activities in 1919. Giap attended a French-run school in Hue that was also attended by Nguyen Sinh Cung (later known as Ho Chi Minh). This was a fortuitous association – these two young men would rise to be the top military and political leaders of the new state of Vietnam forged from over a century of nationalist dissent with French colonial rule. As a young man, Giap became a journalist. He was involved in underground nationalist activities that eventually caught up with him in 1930 when he was arrested and sent to Lao Bao prison in

Quang Tri province for two years. While at Lao Bao he met his first wife, a fellow prisoner. After early release and relocation to Hanoi, Giap became involved with several nationalist publications that were eventually banned by the French authorities. Giap went on to obtain a degree in law and continued subversive activities as a member of the Communist party before being ordered to escape to China to avoid imprisonment. In doing so he was forced to leave behind his wife, Nguyen Thi Quang Thai, and their daughter.

Quang Thai was subsequently arrested by the French and tortured to death at the Hoa Loa prison, a name meaning furnace or oven, in 1941. Hoa Loa saw later prominence as 'the Hanoi Hilton', so named by American prisoners of war during the Vietnam War. A prison for the oppressed became a prison for the oppressors.

In 1941, Giap emerged as the head of the military wing of the Communist party, known as the Viet Minh, when he began to organise locals in an irregular rural force to oppose the French and Japanese. Operations began in the mountainous Vu Nhai district of north-east Vietnam, where several caves provided shelter for covert activity and hideouts from French Vichy patrols. The small initial force carefully integrated with the local populace and over a period of years was able to create a significant local militia that was a forerunner of the North Vietnamese Army. This was a clear distinction from the headlong rush of Che Guevara in the Congo and Bolivia, with the unfortunate ending of both brief campaigns.

Towards the end of World War II, Giap felt it was time to test his nascent army against the French occupying force, which was dispersed among isolated outposts in his area of operations in northern Vietnam. To this end, Giap selected the outpost at Khai Phat, which the French had forcibly occupied from a local Communist sympathiser. To take the post Giap created the first Viet Minh platoon, 34 strong and named after the famous 13th-century Viet hero, Tran Hung Dao, who had repelled several attempted invasions by the Mongols.

In these first acts, Giap followed the well-worn guerrilla template – starting with a small group and a manageable first target that could provide an easy first victory and a beacon to evoke greater local support. Surveillance of the post was conducted by a local boy who reported only one French officer with local soldiers whereupon

General Vo Nguyen Giap, 1954. (Wikimedia Commons)

Giap followed Washington, and attacked on Christmas Day 1944. The French officer was killed, weapons seized and the local soldiers were released after being encouraged to defect to the Viet Minh. This catch-and-release policy effectively drew recruits and projected the movement as being one of the people. Bob Greer considers this the first battle of the Vietnam War.

Giap went on to launch similar successful attacks against the French outposts that took advantage of the war coming to a close and the decline of French and Japanese influence. The Viet Minh emerged as a credible national military force and was given international recognition from the least expected country, the United States of America.

The Vietnamese nationalist movement was sufficiently impressive that at their request in 1945, the precursor to the CIA, the Office of Strategic Services, sent a training group called the Deer team to meet with Giap and Ho Chi Minh. Aside from training the Viet Minh for their actions against the Japanese, the Deer team sought information from Ho Chi Minh, who confirmed their Communist affiliation. The Deer team trained the Viet Minh in the use of various American small arms supplied by them for a short while before the Japanese surrender.

The French resumed control of Vietnam after the war despite Ho Chi Minh's declaration of independence in Hanoi on 2 September 1945 to create the Democratic Republic of Vietnam. This declaration was largely ignored by world powers.

The success of a guerrilla movement in no small part depends on an earnest desire to create an **independent democratic state** such as that envisaged by Washington, Bolivar, Koos De La Rey and Mao on the cusp of their guerrilla campaigns. An insurgency predicated on religious divisions, ignoring election results or subsisting on mayhem financed by criminal acts will not survive. Examples of these failed attempts include UNITA during the 27-year Angolan civil war, the FARC of Colombia for over fifty years and the Sandinistas of Nicaragua who were forced into support of a democratic state now recently in jeopardy.

By 1946 the French had resumed control of Vietnam and despite numerous negotiations, the Indochina War broke out after the French shelled Haiphong harbour killing thousands. Giap was now Minister of Defence for a government in waiting and experienced conventional war for the first time. French forces employed air, land and naval power to overwhelm the Viet Minh and this low-level conflict continued until late 1953 when French General Henri-Eugene Navarre took over command of French forces and decided to restrict Viet Minh access routes to China and Laos by constructing a series of outposts or 'hedgehogs' around an old Japanese air strip in the valley known as Dien Bien Phu. This location was in a bowl surrounded by thick jungle-covered hills, prone to flooding in the monsoon and only capable of resupply by air. Over the objections of his subordinates, Navarre commenced airdrops of over 10,000 French soldiers that were dispersed around seven outposts surrounding the landing strip. The mistaken French thinking was that these fortifications would draw the Viet Minh into a mass attack where they could be destroyed by superior French artillery and air power.

Ho Chi Minh saw that allowing the French to surrender would give the political advantage at any future negotiating table and Giap was ordered to eliminate the French presence at Dien Bien Phu. By January 1954 the Viet Minh had encircled the French with over 50,000 troops and artillery before buying into the French narrative on bad Chinese advice and starting mass attacks on the French encampments. These failed miserably and thousands of Viet Minh soldiers were lost. This was not entirely Giap's fault as he was being pushed to secure a quick victory to enhance the Vietnamese position at the Geneva conference, which was scheduled to begin that May.

The situation was not as perilous as it first seemed for the Vietnamese guerrillas. The major international French force had been self-deceived into seeking a one-punch result after an extended low-intensity conflict based on a number of inaccurate presumptions namely: that they could be re-supplied by air; that the Viet Minh would mass attack into non-existence; and the Viet Minh were far from Hanoi with limited supply.

The new strategy by Giap was less conventional in nature; the slow erosion of French capability by significant artillery strikes, multiple sniper attacks and trench works. China was a strong supporter of the Viet Minh at this time and started to supply 37mm anti-aircraft guns with trained Vietnamese operators. This was combined with numerous sniper units to disrupt French troop movements and lower their morale. At great cost in human effort, artillery was placed uphill in emplacement protected by thick jungle. These rained shells on the French airstrip from many angles, rendering it unusable. This strategy can be compared to the South African siege of the Cuito Cuanavale air strip during the Angola civil war in 1978 – hundreds of shells landed every day, forcing the opposing troops underground, an option unavailable to the French in the sodden earth at Dien Bien Phu.

Assisted by Chinese engineers, the Viet Minh constructed hundreds of miles of trenches that approached French outposts without disruption from their artillery fire while allowing attacks at several points. Further Chinese supply of artillery and ammunition ramped up the onslaught and in March 1954 the final offensive began. The pressure was so great that the French artillery commander, Colonel Charles Piroth, committed suicide on 15 March.

The landing strip was destroyed very early in the final offensive and the French were forced into air supply to a much-reduced perimeter meaning that only half the needed supplies could be dropped in each day, and much of that fell into the hands of the Viet Minh. Destruction of air capability meant increased casualty mortality as there was no evacuation ability and even water was in short supply. Ultimately Viet Minh reinforcement approached one-half of their entire capacity while the French had only committed one-fifth of their army in Vietnam. The four to one Viet Minh artillery superiority soon eliminated French artillery, which then opened the door to mass ground attacks.

The attack ended with a French surrender on 7 May 1954. The cost to the French was over 20,000 dead, wounded or captured as well as 35 aircraft shot down. Of the nearly 40,000 French prisoners taken by the Viet Minh during the Indochina War, only a little over 10,000 survived.

The victory at Dien Bien Phu was to be the greatest military achievement of Giap, who had had to implement policy directives from Vietnamese and Chinese leadership into practical steps on the ground. This was the closest that a guerrilla force ever came to engaging in a conventional war but it was a unique set of circumstances where the battle was forced on them by a foreign power that did not realise the level of support the Chinese were giving – the introduction of artillery at Dien Bien Phu was a game changer. The Viet Minh kept up the pressure even after Dien Bien Phu and peace negotiations with the destruction of the retreating French GM 100 unit at Mang Yang Pass that resulted in nearly 2,000 killed, wounded or captured.

The French departed shortly thereafter, leaving behind a country divided into North and South. The presence of US military advisors to the Army of South Vietnam escalated to troop deployments in 1965 after the Gulf of Tonkin incident. Various skirmishes between the North Vietnamese Army (NVA) and Viet Cong irregulars in the south with US forces led to the battle of the Ia Drang Valley in 1965.

The NVA under General Giap sought to cut a major road at Pleiku located in difficult terrain that would effectively divide South Vietnam. At that time the US strategy was air mobility, deploying a quick reaction force utilising several hundred technologically advanced helicopters, gunships, artillery and bombers. In October

The Viet Minh were the political and military group prior to French departure. The **North Vietnamese Army (NVA)** was the formal army of North Vietnam after the French departure. The **Viet Cong (VC)**, meaning Vietnamese Communists, was a name given to irregular North Vietnamese guerrillas in South Vietnam by US soldiers.

1965 the NVA attacked a US Special Forces camp at Plei Mei before retreating to the hills surrounding the valley. This led to a full-scale air assault that initially faltered as the NVA attacked the landing area at sufficiently close range to temporarily negate artillery and air strikes. The initial attacks having been repulsed, the US commander showered the NVA with mass artillery and air strikes that caused casualties in the thousands to hundreds on the US side. The NVA retreated into Cambodia leaving Giap with a well-earned lesson in US tactics.

General Giap's costly education at Ia Drang and his experience at Dien Bien Phu were not forgotten when he next encountered the US forces. During the summer of 1967 the NVA stepped up attacks at a US firebase at Khe Sanh in Quang Tri province roughly midway between North and South Vietnam and located a few miles from the border with Laos. These attacks were part of a strategy to draw American troops from urban areas. The ultimate objective was to inflict a significant body count to deter the American incursion both in the war zone and at home. Another goal was the drawing of US military assets into rural areas in preparation for the NVA Tet offensive on South Vietnamese cities in January 1968.

Like the South African incursion at Cuito Cuanavale in Angola at the end of 1987, the objective was to pin down enemy troops and create political heat. Not every offensive must have an end game of capture, and certainly attacks can be Trojan horses that defy real-time analysis. This is where the value from the present-day evolution of warrior academics and philosophers such as former US General David Petraeus can be appreciated with

US Army combat operations in Ia Drang Valley, Vietnam, November 1965. (US Army/Wikimedia Commons)

multi-dimensional thinking, especially in the Middle East trend of religious and tribal conflicts.

American forces on the ground in the recently captured Khe Sanh base only numbered 6,000 but over 45,000 were concentrated nearby in border provinces. General Giap had an almost equal number of troops divided between Khe Sanh and nearby areas as well as over 200 artillery pieces, mortars and rockets all directed at the firebase. Mobile NVA mortar teams and snipers pinned down the Marines on the base while making counter-fire extremely difficult and even detonated tons of stored ammunition. Despite intense bombardment on both sides, along with air strikes in the tens of thousands of tons of bombs, the base was not overrun during six months of battle. The Americans eventually evacuated the base in June 1968 still under NVA fire. The ghost of Dien Bien Phu blinded the American leadership whose core beliefs did not comprehend high casualties as a war strategy, even while Vietnamese leadership repeatedly proclaimed that victories were not important but how much suffering the Americans would endure before departure – a concept now adopted by Islamic extremists who do not see a soldier, but an accurate long-range missile in the form of IED vests.

The NVA launched the Tet Offensive during the Vietnamese New Year, 1968, simultaneously attacking occupied towns and cities throughout South Vietnam, including Hue. The siege of Hue lasted several months and resulted in thousands of civilian deaths but the real effect was on the American public who lost confidence in the US government and its strategy in Vietnam, leading to protracted negotiations for peace. The military strategy of General Giap, however costly, was translated into political power that eventually overwhelmed the mighty US military not on the battlefield but at the negotiating table leading to the Paris Peace Accords in 1973.

A great guerrilla leader must of necessity absorb significant, even exorbitant, losses to fulfil the greater end of a free nation. Premier in this category was General Giap whose nation suffered over a million casualties to resist French and American occupation. After the death of Ho Chi Minh in 1969, Giap's star began to wane and he was eventually reduced to fill a succession of lesser posts until retirement in 1991 and death in 2013.

CHAPTER 8

MANUEL MARULANDA, COLOMBIA

Manuel Marulanda Velez, the war name or alias of one of the oldest serving guerrilla leaders, lived a long life and died of natural causes in March 2008. He was first known as Pedro Antonio Marin and later, Tirofijo, his nickname meaning 'sure shot'. He was the most famous leader of the Revolutionary Armed Forces of Colombia or Fuerzas Armadas Revolucionarias de Colombia-Ejército del Pueblo (FARC). The name 'Manuel Marulanda' was a dead man's name that he took as an alias after one of many reports that he had been killed. The name of Tirofijo by one account was due to his predilection for performing the coup de grâce shot to the head of his target as opposed to being a good shot.

He was born to a large Liberal-supporting rural peasant family sometime between 1928 and 1930 before ending up as a Liberal guerrilla during the conflict with Conservatives in what became known as the La Violencia period in Colombia's history that started with the assassination of Liberal President Jorge Gaitan on 9 April 1948. Thereafter, members of the Marin family had seized the town of Ceilan in the south-western Valle Del Cauca department of Colombia before fleeing from an attack by Conservative forces. Tirofijo was still a teenager when he enlisted in the Liberal guerrilla or self-defence movement in that rural area as the peasants sought to protect themselves from roaming Conservative paramilitary squads who left behind a trail of violence. Remarkably, these groups still persist today in the costume of narco-terrorists.

There was a short period of peace and stability when the Liberal and Conservative movements signed a national pact in 1956. Further attacks by army and paramilitary elements sent Tirofijo and his small band of followers into the mountains where the Republic of Marquetalia in the southern Tolima department of west central Colombia was declared in 1961. This was followed by several other republics throughout Colombia who sought to separate themselves from oppression and government control.

Tirofijo had by this time joined the Communist Party, and after a period of time, rose to join the leadership in Tolima. He went on to head the military wing of the Communist Party which evolved into the Revolutionary Armed Forces of Colombia (FARC), a guerrilla group that still exists, in a more demilitarised and political form. The FARC, also referred to as the Southern Bloc, was co-founded with Jacobo Arenas who was the ideological leader but subordinate to Marulanda, for whom he had the greatest regard.

In May 1964, the Marquetalia group faced the challenge of a government offensive that resulted in the nascent FARC guerrillas slipping away along a pre-prepared escape route, despite the efforts of several thousand government troops and bombing sorties. Colombian army leadership grudgingly admitted the skilled manner in which the group had outmanoeuvred the attack. It was not to be an isolated event. This was a small victory – the retreat of a new guerrilla force facing a large, experienced army contingent that only enhanced the former's reputation, leading to increased support from the local inhabitants.

The group and their families then temporarily moved some 25 miles to another self-declared republic, that of Rio Chiquito in the Cauca department before another Colombian army raid sent

The **lesson** here for students of counter-insurgency is that the prevention of early small victories of a budding revolt can be the most important tactic. This will require prescient leadership along with inordinate resources incapable of logical explanation to political oversight.

them deeper into the wilderness of Meta and Caqueta. This strategy of moving frequently into unpopulated arears far from government control became a way of life for decades. They were able to maintain a camp for the FARC leadership – known as Casa Verde near La Uribe in the Meta department – that remained unknown to the Colombian military from 1965 until 1990.

The Marquetalia group created the FARC in 1966 and commenced decades of guerrilla strike and retreat actions, although they were unable to maintain control of any significant territory due to the pressure from an active government military. The FARC were restricted to south-west Colombia and mainly their heartland, the department of Cauca. An attempt to open a second front and move further west into the coffee-rich and former Tirofijo home department of Quindio in the 1970s failed because of numerous debilitating attacks by the Colombian army. The FARC numbered fewer a thousand fighters at that time, a size which was fairly constant for the previous decade.

One early success came in February 1977 when a large group of FARC guerrillas took over the entire town of La Macarena in the Meta region, seizing government buildings, the local police chief and the biggest prize of all, Richard Starr, a U.S. Peace Corps worker. Starr was held until 1980 and this template for operations was repeated numerous times by the FARC in the following decades.

A pivotal turning point for the FARC came during the 1980s when the older FARC leadership began to include younger men such as Raul Reyes, Mono Jojoy and Ivan Rios. The FARC realised that to grow required resources so they commenced an unrelenting series of kidnappings, involvement in the drug trade and extortion to finance expansion not only in numbers but to open new fronts, including in urban areas. The new source of funding would also facilitate training camps and social programmes in areas under their control.

In this, Tirofijo showed some elements of a successful guerrilla leader. The necessity of evolution in tactics and ideology, the sensibility of succession planning with the inclusion not only of younger men who had risen through the ranks, such as Mono Jojoy, but academics such as Alfonso Cano.

Alfonso Cano during peace talks with the government of Cesar Gaviria, 1 February 1990. (Salvador Cano/Wikimedia Commons)

One of the earliest kidnappings, which foretold of difficulties to come was the 1975 kidnapping of Dutch Honorary Consul of Cali, Eric Leupin, for a claimed ransom of USD 1 million. The refusal of any official negotiation and the subsequent arrest of his wife for attempting to deliver a reduced amount of USD 50,000 saw him remaining in captivity until October 1976. The FARC continued annual increases in kidnapping, reaching a staggering 3,000 in 2000, which suggests not only many millions of dollars in ransoms but a logistical problem to maintain such large numbers in captivity across Colombia in secrecy. This unsustainable volume, a product of excess success, may have helped to push the FARC to the negotiating table.

US senator Dianne Feinstein stated in June 2000 that the FARC held up to 2,500 hostages of whom 500 were military and police with the remainder being many high-profile individuals. She went on to state that the FARC enjoyed income of USD 2–3 million a day from involvement in drug, mainly cocaine, trafficking.

The 1982 election victory of Conservative Colombian President Belisario Betancur provided an opportunity for Manuel Marulanda, as the Colombian government offered amnesty to Colombian guerrillas, allowing them to rejoin mainstream society, a sentiment that received the personal endorsement of the FARC chief. Betancur went on to pass an amnesty law that was taken up by some guerrillas but mainly acted as an engine towards establishing dialogue with the FARC. In 1984, negotiations with Marulanda commenced in the FARC heartland of La Uribe and ended with a cease-fire declaration.

Any successful guerrilla movement has to have an objective of transition to mainstream society and participation in the political system by having a political wing. The list of movements with a political wing is long; including for example Sinn Fein of the Irish Republican Army of Northern Ireland, the Basque party Batasuna and ETA of Spain, the Kurdistan Workers' Party in Turkey and the YPG in Syria. To this end the FARC created the Patriotic Union in May 1985 which had some success in elections but was thwarted by the murders of several thousand members and two of its presidential candidates, the last in 1990. By June 1987 the FARC ended the cease fire with an attack on a Colombian Army unit in Caqueta department in the south that killed 27 soldiers. History is now dangerously close to repeating itself.

The transformation of the FARC from a small rural guerrilla group constantly on the run in 1966 to a multi-front force that ran in the thousands with a large area under their control was nothing short of miraculous. The changes in finance and strategy were either due to the policies of Manuel Marulanda or the influence of younger men who had joined the leadership. Analysts believed that the FARC objectives were threefold by 1990:

1. To control the coca-growing regions and the revenue from that trade.
2. Expand across the country to increase the operational area of FARC, which would thin the Colombian armed forces.
3. Reduce central government control by regular roadblocks on roads leading to outside regions from the capital.

In 1990, while negotiations were still ongoing between the FARC and the Colombian government, Jacobo Arenas died of natural causes at the Casa Verde compound. Shortly after, in December 1990, the Colombian forces raided Casa Verde causing over one hundred casualties but as always, the FARC leadership made a disciplined retreat before resuming multiple daily attacks throughout Colombia. Tirofijo and the FARC, enhanced by improved finances and several thousand fighters on many fronts, created a string of major military victories and skirmishes with Colombian forces.

On 30 August 1996, a surprise night attack on the Las Delicias military base in isolated Putumayo near the borders with Ecuador and Peru resulted in over 100 soldiers killed, wounded or captured. The FARC had conducted extensive surveillance before a sustained attack of 15 hours leaving the base totally destroyed. One report stated that it took six and a half hours, with many transport changes, before reinforcements were able to reach the base in circumstances where the number and identities of Colombian soldiers taken prisoner, or their likely location, were unknown.

In March 1998, a FARC force of several hundred ambushed and substantially destroyed the Colombian Army's 3rd Mobile Brigade, a counter-insurgency unit, at El Billar in Caqueta, causing losses of 107 of 154 government soldiers. Poor intelligence, limited equipment, bad weather, limited air cover and the difficult terrain were blamed but the FARC had carefully selected a target after extensive intelligence gathering before the trap was sprung.

In August 1998, FARC guerrillas attacked and destroyed a Colombian army anti-drug base at Miraflores in Guaviare. In November 1998, a thousand FARC guerrillas captured Mitu, the provincial capital of Vaupes in the Amazon basin. The guerrillas were able to hold their conquest for three days until the Colombian forces received permission to use nearby Brazilian airbases. At this time Tirofijo gave the unfailing impression that the Colombian government was under siege and the FARC could strike at will.

A perfect opportunity, greater than any military victory, for Tirofijo to outmanoeuvre the entire Colombian government, was handed to him when President-Elect Andres Pastrana secretly visited Tirofijo in person, in June 1998 to discuss peace negotiations. A tentative agreement was made for the FARC to be given a demilitarised zone amounting to over 42,000 square kilometres in southern Colombia while peace talks continued. Marulanda used the hiatus in operations in the FARC-controlled zone to recruit more troops and expand cocaine revenue operations while still holding many prisoners and hostages.

Peace was not to last and the FARC continued attacks involving thousands of guerrillas in July 1999 against military bases and government administration sites in Meta, Gauviare, Huila, Putumayo and Caqueta provinces. One shocking skirmish that July saw FARC rebels overrun an army camp near Gutierrez, 27 miles from Bogota in Colombia's eastern cordillera, resulting in 36 dead government soldiers. By January 2000, hundreds of emboldened FARC guerrillas attacked the towns of Une, Quetame and Guayabetal less than 30 miles from Bogota. This was followed in October when the FARC occupied the town of Dabeida, killing 54 soldiers and policemen including 22 onboard a Blackhawk helicopter downed by FARC fire. Delayed reinforcement and rescue were mostly for logical reasons, Blackhawk Down, Somalia revisited.

There was a hiatus in these frenetic guerrilla raids in 2000 as the Colombian government and their combined military forces or FMC underwent a period of introspection and transformation – the cornerstone of any effective counter-insurgency, the ability to evolve promptly to significant shifts in the battlefield after conventional tactics repeatedly fail. The FMC implemented the following:

1. The efficient management of intelligence and battlefield reports, both long term and real time, to be used in a meaningful manner utilising directed air strikes in conjunction with troop movements.

2. A rapid reaction force of several thousand, with deployment capability using elite troops with night vision equipment.

3. Increased signal intelligence to fill the vacuum of limited human intelligence in guerrilla territory.

FMC attacks on the FARC increased almost threefold in 2000 with FARC casualties of almost six hundred, nearly double the figure for the previous year, but the FARC attack on Dabeida reminded the Colombian government that the FARC core capability remained untouched.

The lesson here perhaps is that huge outside aid, in the billions, against an entrenched locally supported guerrilla group with massive government military assets deployed in the field, can best hope for a stalemate to provide an opportunity for realistic political options. The FARC remained undiminished by renewed attacks of the Colombian military.

There was further escalation by the FARC in the use of a new terror weapon to the Colombian civil conflict, namely, inaccurate propane tank bombs lobbed into rural towns. In May 2002, one such action in the village of Bella Vista in Choco department saw a propane bomb

President of Colombia, Alvaro Uribe, 2004.
(US Government/Wikimedia Commons)

thrown through the local church roof, killing over 100 civilians who had been seeking safety in a traditional conflict sanctuary.

2002 also saw the FARC hijack a domestic plane to seize Senator Jorge Gechem Turbay, who would not be released for six years. The Pastrana government belatedly terminated the peace negotiations and closed the FARC demilitarisation zone. Shortly thereafter presidential candidate Ingrid Betancourt was kidnapped by FARC on a highway while on the campaign trail. The following April, FARC kidnapped 12 lawmakers from Cali, 11 of whom were killed in 2007.

The FARC activities came to a screeching halt in August 2002 when the first true match for the FARC arrived, the iron man of Colombia, Alvaro Uribe, who ascended to power on a mandate to crush FARC. No more peace treaties or demilitarised zones, just war for breakfast, war for lunch and war for dinner. Uribe's own father had been killed during an attempted FARC kidnapping almost two decades earlier. The Colombian president had survived several assassination attempts including FARC mortar bombing of his inaugural ceremony.

Assisted by nearly a billion dollars of American financial aid known as Plan Colombia, some of which was for social programmes, Uribe increased security personnel between 2002 and 2010 to over 1,000 municipalities. Kidnappings were reduced from thousands annually to just a couple hundred with the FARC area of operation severely limited to isolated jungle areas with a halving of their membership to under 10,000.

A crucial lynchpin of Uribe's strategy was the demobilisation of guerrilla fighters – numbered more than 11,000 – between 2002 and 2008. Smartly recruiting an advertising agency who discerned after multiple interviews with former guerrillas that soccer matches were the best medium to promote a warm reception for guerrillas that wished to defect, the government distributed flyers in conjunction with radio and television advertisements during prominent soccer games. Guerrillas who opted for this way out were quickly put on air to promote more defections, some of which sought to capitalise on rewards for FARC commanders. This ploy led to the death of FARC leader Ivan Rios in March 2008, by his own security chief who carried the severed hand of his former leader to the Colombian government as proof of the assassination, collecting a bounty of $2.5 million, a first for the Colombian government.

Against this backdrop, the early advantages of the Pastrana demilitarised zone began to dissipate with the election of Uribe, the retraction of the FARC and most importantly, a wholesale turn of public opinion against the conflict. The elderly Marulanda, whether punch-drunk from the Uribe administration or simply fearful of an Ivan Rios or Raul Reyes ending earlier that March, died of natural causes on 26 March 2008.

Tirofijo died on the cusp of an extended programme of targeted assassinations of the FARC leadership by the FMC that included Raul Reyes in March 2008, Mono Jojoy in 2010, Alfonso Cano in 2011, Danilo Garcia in 2012 and Roman Ruiz in 2015. In this, the FMC took a page from the well-worn Israeli counter-insurgency play book with a plan that eventually drove FARC to the negotiating table and a peace treaty. Another ploy, the payment of high rewards,

On 2 July 2008, Uribe's most daring accomplishment received world-wide acclaim with the extended deception rescue pioneered by the Colombian forces known as Operation *Jaque*, acknowledged as a strategy that not only had no US involvement, but was a case where student became teacher. Twelve unarmed Colombian soldiers pretending to be Red Cross workers were able to rescue 15 FARC hostages including Ingrid Betancourt and three Americans, plus capture a FARC commander. The year-long operation, led by Colombian Army General Freddy Padilla, had its genesis in a turned FARC commander, an increasingly common occurrence, who was able to convince another FARC commander, Geraldo Aguilar or Cesar, the captor of high-value hostages in Guaviare department of Southern Colombia, to release them to two faux Red Cross helicopters. The ruse was complete with the hostages put in restraints, fake Red Cross workers wearing Che Guevara shirts, and Cesar joining the trip with another guerrilla. As a backup, 2,000 helicopter-borne Colombian troops were on standby and nearby in the event a forceful rescue became necessary. The operation also benefited from advanced surveillance sensors for several months prior that were likely unknown to the isolated FARC guerrillas. This was the greatest embarrassment to FARC command and control in its history, best described by General Padilla as mainly due to the medieval state of FARC communications. Tirofijo was not around to experience the FARC's greatest debacle.

Almost eight years later came the 2016 successful peace treaty with the FARC by President Juan Manuel Santos which has seen significant implementation with demobilisation camps and even training for former FARC guerrillas to become bodyguards for FARC political candidates who fear a Patriotic Union redux of murders and intimidation. As in many things guerrilla, only time will tell.

CHAPTER 9

JONAS SAVIMBI, ANGOLA

One of the most ferocious guerrilla leaders ever unleashed on the world arose out of the civil war in Angola. Between 1975 and 2002, Jonas Malheiro Savimbi waged a masterful guerrilla campaign for 27 years, a period probably eclipsed only by the FARC rebels of Colombia.

Born in Munhango, Bie province on 3 August 1934, he spent most of his guerrilla years between Bie and the nearby province of Moxico where he was eventually hunted and killed in 2002 by the ruling MPLA government army known as FAPLA (Forcas Armadas Populares de Libertacao de Angola) now FAA (Forcas Armadas Angolanas). Originally known as Portuguese West Africa the country's name was changed to Angola in the early 1950s with the provinces of Bie and Moxico being measured in hundreds of thousands of square kilometres. The remote location from the coast and major cities caused early Portuguese settlers to call it the land at the end of the earth.

The common story is that his father, Lote Savimbi, was a stationmaster along the Benguela railway which ran, when first built in 1912, from the port cities of Lobito and Benguela to Huambo in the interior. Lote was moved several times due to his active participation in Protestant churches as a preacher in a mainly Catholic country. These inconvenient displacements not only led a young Jonas to observe the oratorical prowess of his father but also develop a keen knowledge of Angolan geography and the main transportation system. Most accounts of Savimbi's father's life neglect the family history of his grandfather, an Ovimbundu tribal chief dispossessed after a failed 1902 uprising against the Portuguese colonialists. This may have driven Savimbi to the point of history repeating itself in 2002, when he ultimately failed to overthrow the ruling MPLA government and was killed, whereupon his few remaining followers dispersed or surrendered.

His father's church affiliation proved useful when Savimbi later obtained a scholarship from the United Church of Christ to study medicine at the University of Lisbon after graduating at the top of his high school class. In 1958 Lisbon, Jonas had what one newspaper report described as outstanding scholastic achievement matched by a miserable social life. As a dark-skinned student among the lighter mixed elite who received the majority of government scholarships, he never felt more out of place.

Nevertheless, this did not stop him from displaying his nascent political ambitions by becoming a student activist in the budding Angola independence movement. His activities caught the attention of future independence leader Agostinho Neto and leader of National Liberation Front of Angola (FNLA), Holden Roberto, in 1961. Roberto had initially formed the Union of Peoples of Northern Angola (UPNA), then the Union of Peoples of Angola (UPA) before the FNLA. It was the UPA that Savimbi joined as a student, although it was a Bakongo tribe-dominated faction which later caused his estrangement. The FNLA later became notorious for their farcical recruitment of foreign mercenaries, 13 of whom were tried in Luanda in 1976 by the ruling Movimento Popular de Libertacao de Angola (MPLA) with four being executed, including their leader, the vicious Costas Georgiou. This was merely political drama for the world stage that soon paled in comparison with the ongoing fight with the well-supplied and -organised UNITA. It also ignored the fact that the MPLA subsisted on revenue from Gulf Oil of the USA, a country which was providing material support to Savimibi.

Savimbi came from the large Ovimbundu tribe, which at that time amounted to over a third of the population of Angola and this

Jonas Savimbi, 1989. (Emmuhl/ Wikimedia Commons)

provided him with a lasting power base in Moxico. Another reason for his movement away from the UPA, and ultimately from Lisbon, was the attention he drew from the Portuguese secret police who not only contacted him, but pressured him to cooperate against the Angolan pro-independence community.

It was during this period that Savimbi left Portugal and became a student, still in medicine, at the University of Fribourg in Switzerland before he switched academic pursuits to international law and politics at Lausanne University. There he impressed at least one professor with his grasp of geopolitics before supposedly emerging with a doctorate in political science in 1965. There have been several differing media reports on the subject of his doctorate and at least one states that it was never awarded. Nevertheless he was referred to and wished to be addressed as Dr. Jonas Savimbi from that time on.

In July 1964, Savimbi left his position as head of foreign affairs for FNLA after developing sufficient contacts with one of his future benefactors, China. After failing to secure support in Eastern Europe, he travelled to Nanking, China in 1965 with a few supporters to study guerrilla warfare for four months. China had promised training and financial support but ultimately was unable to supply weapons due to logistical problems. In China, he became strongly influenced by Maoism, especially the concepts of self-reliance and the conduct of guerrilla warfare wherein leadership was within the country. This worked well in a large and mostly ungovernable Angola as opposed to a well-regulated country like South Africa which saw the guerrilla leadership mostly confined to prison or friendly neighbouring countries.

Savimbi returned to Angola in 1966 when he rejected MPLA overtures to start his own group with Antonio da Costa Fernandes, the Uniao Nacional para a Independencia Total de Angola or the National Union for the Total Independence of Angola (UNITA). According to one account, UNITA was officially founded on 13 March 1966 in the remote village of Muangai, Moxico province. Co-founder Antonio da Costa Fernandes, who was at one time Savimbi's closest confidant and ally, documented the founding of UNITA in the less remote but more distant Champaix, Switzerland as October of 1963. After four years in Egypt and a brief period in the field, Fernandes occupied a number of UNITA foreign affairs posts. In February 1992, ten years to the month before the death of Savimbi, he defected to the MPLA government where he held a succession of diplomatic posts.

Unlike the urbanised intellectuals and mesticos of the MPLA, Savimbi's UNITA was put forward for the black peasants but also emphasised in its constitution the proportional representation of all Angolans. Although lacking in trained cadres like the MPLA, UNITA quickly spread throughout the Ovimbundo heartland under the uncontested pyramid leadership of Savimbi who utilised a Maoist formula of local village councils that reported to a political commissar, who in turn reported to a central committee. This system worked sufficiently well among the mostly illiterate and sparsely populated peasantry that the movement spread widely and eastwards until it encountered MPLA cadres doing exactly the same thing. UNITA encouraged food cooperatives among the villagers and unlike many similar experiments outside Angola, under the strongman Savimbi it worked reasonably well.

At the time of independence in 1975, UNITA controlled most of the rural population east of Luanda as well as much of the food-producing territory. Savimbi and UNITA were well poised at the time of independence as a formidable, well organised party. Independence came much quicker than anticipated for Angola

Teixeira de Sousa railway station, Angola, c. 1960 (Jose Campos)

with the 1974 military coup in Portugal known as the Carnation Revolution, taken from the flowers put into the barrels of rifles of army soldiers on the streets by protestors.

Much earlier, UNITA had launched their first attack on Portuguese rulers with an attack on the Benguela railway at Luau then Teixeira de Sousa in December 1966. Copper ore shipments from Zambia and Zaire were halted for a week as a result of this armed disruption.

Savimbi frequently took on friends of diametrically opposite politics. The railway attack was followed by a long association with the USA after he received military training from China and later on to an association with apartheid South Africa. Between 1966 and 1975, Savimbi moved through Zambia several times in a clandestine manner and was also expelled on occasion by the government, when it became upset at the interruption of copper revenue by the UNITA blockade of the Benguela railway on two occasions in 1967. At this time Savimbi was secretly dealing with Portuguese military intelligence to fight the MPLA in any way possible in eastern Angola and the central highlands, a position that continued until the 1974 coup by leftist army officers, the very contradiction in terms.

Like many guerrilla leaders Savimbi followed a recipe of establishing a personality cult, creating a continuous atmosphere

Jonas Savimbi at Jamba, Angola, 26 May 1990. Tito Chingunji, seen just behind Savimbi, was not saved by the respect and friendship for him among the US liaison contacts with UNITA. (Fred Oelschig)

of paranoia engendered by the occasional blood-letting of high officials and lowly supporters alike, destroying actual and perceived competitors for leadership and having multiple alliances that he betrayed frequently. Unlike many independence guerrilla movements led by a group of leaders with differing responsibilities or fraternal connections such as the Sandinistas of Nicaragua, Savimbi not only distanced himself ideologically from his initial supporters but literally cut off many of the higher echelons of his group. Over the years he developed a leadership methodology based on an incalculable combination of fear, superstition, whim, betrayal, jealousy and ultimately overconfidence that included keeping families of his associates as virtual hostages at his headquarters in Jamba and elsewhere. This pattern, however distasteful, allowed him to survive as a leader for 27 years. Some of the UNITA leadership who fell victim to his methods included: Pedro 'Tito' Chingunji, UNITA Foreign Affairs Secretary, executed 1991; General Antero Vieira Menzes, executed 13 April 1999; General Julio Armindo (Tarzan), executed 13 April 1999;

General Fernando Elias Bandua, executed 13 April 1999; General Assobio de Bala, executed 13 April 1999; General Daniel Fuma, executed 13 April 1999; Brigadier Peres Jonas (Grito), executed 13 April 1999; Colonel Bernard Sombongo, executed 13 April 1999; and Commander Jorge Sangumba, executed 1991.

After the civil war began in 1975, subsequent to Angolan independence, Savimbi's MPLA opponents took up with the Soviets and their Cuban counterparts in a most earnest fashion for military support that included a significant personnel presence of technical advisors in the country that trickled down to the battlefield. Savimbi then cut off his Chinese benefactors in favour of the USA and apartheid South Africa whilst declaring himself an anti-communist.

Savimbi enjoyed a period of relative calm until 1980 as the MPLA confronted a shortage of military might that the Soviets sought to relieve by a multi-billion-dollar supply of arms, equipment, advisors and Cuban troops in the field. The MPLA also had some internal dissension in 1977 which was quickly put down by their leader Agostinho Neto who followed up with a period of opposition cleansing that caused a delay in a concerted attack on UNITA, post election. When Neto died in 1979 his appointed successor, Jose Dos Santos, became the new leader.

Savimbi and Dos Santos were not dissimilar in that their major strength was political organisation, survival and seeing off potential rivals while remaining in power. In this, Savimbi was more in the mould of Mao or Ho Chi Minh, being the overall commander setting policy and objectives while having a military leadership that implemented orders. Ho Chi Minh had the brilliant General Giap and Savimbi had many good field commanders including his nephew, known as General Ben Ben, and the former chief of staff of the Angola military, Geraldo Sachipengo Nunda, both of whom defected from UNITA.

The genius of Savimbi lay in his ability not only to speak several languages but to regularly engage the international community to search for and maintain support for UNITA in the Angolan civil war. His major ally in this endeavour was the highly proficient South African Defence Force that undertook many invasions, incursions and attacks in Angola between 1975 and 1988, effectively propping up UNITA in Angola and even saving them from decimation.

Savimbi used American financial support to create a modern guerrilla army that included regular soldiers, militia and specialist units. These were effectively orchestrated to control vast swathes of eastern Angola and the highlands while conducting ambushes and sabotage deep in the government-controlled territory of Angola. As I noted in my book on Angola: 'This bizarre situation was that UNITA troops financed by the USA attacked assets of a US corporation Gulf Oil in Angola, protected by Cuban soldiers, paid by the Angola government from oil revenue from the selfsame US corporation. The dollar was mightier than conscience or common sense'.

Savimbi was sufficiently close to the action or important enough a target that he was wounded on some occasions although confirmation of this is very sparse. There was an air raid on his headquarters of Jamba in eastern Angola on 24 February 1990 when he may have been wounded. Nevertheless it is difficult to identify a battle of the Angolan civil war conflict that occurred without the support and initiative of forces outside Angola, that included the Soviets, Cubans and South Africans over time.

Unlike other guerrilla leaders who fought set-piece battles that put them on the path to national leadership, this scenario eluded Savimbi for over 26 years of civil war, the closest he came was the battle of Cuito Cuanavale.

Savimbi was a guerrilla leader with great organisational abilities that were evident throughout the many years he fought the Angolan government, whose leaders were safely ensconced in Luanda surrounded by Soviet and Cuban protectors. The longevity of UNITA was buttressed by a policy of UNITA commanders making the bush their home. The military wing of UNITA was virtually created from scratch and evolved into a substantial force with many facets over time aided in no small part by the South African advisors and benefactors of UNITA. A 1997 United Nations report put the number of UNITA soldiers that showed up for demobilisation at almost 8,000 while a 2002 report increased this to 80,000 UNITA soldiers after the death of Savimbi.

In a model of equal opportunity Savimbi also created a unit of 50 women soldiers led by female officers in 1987 who joined a military force that for the most part was unpaid and voluntary – though in theory only as coercive measures were often adopted for recruitment.

UNITA also had a radio station called Voz Resistencia do Galo Negro, the Voice of the Resistance of the Black Cockerel, which was believed to consist of four ex-USA military mobile broadcast containers. The majority of content was centred around simple songs and morality skits designed to raise consciousness of the UNITA struggle. In this they were very similar to guerrilla movements worldwide seeking to reach out to a largely rural and illiterate population.

The UNITA training facility at Jamba in eastern Angola included several training camps with six-month cycles that produced about 8,000 troops annually. The main camp was well equipped with generator, hospital, troop barracks and equipment maintenance areas. The troops were given intensive physical, tactical and weaponry training mostly for the AK-47 assault rifle and PKM machine guns. According to SADF Senior Liaison officer Colonel Fred Oelschig, in 1989 UNITA troop strengths included nine regular battalions of 800 men consisting of three infantry companies with five platoons each. A support company consisted of an 81mm mortar platoon, an anti-tank platoon with rocket-propelled grenades (RPG) and a heavy machine-gun platoon. UNITA also had as many as 20 irregular battalions armed with mortars, RPGs and light machine guns, each about 250 men strong.

There was also an UNITA artillery battalion trained with 120mm mortars, 122mm howitzers, 107mm multiple rocket launchers and any other captured FAPLA artillery as well as special units trained to perform reconnaissance, special engineers for demolitions and special anti-aircraft groups who were trained to shoot down FAPA aircraft.

As to equipment, in a videoed interview with the Canadian Ambassador Fowler in 2000, UNITA General Jacinto Ricardo Bandua reported that:

> I held the post of chief of logistics for strategic equipment. UNITA bought a lot of material and many devices – tanks, mortars, mortar

Captured FAPLA T-55 tank with UNITA soldiers, November 1987. (Roland De Vries)

grenades, cannon, launching pads for missiles, ammunition and UNITA also bought a lot of tank accessories. These accessories made it possible for UNITA to rehabilitate the tanks it had captured over the sixteen years of war. Let me say here that over the sixteen years of struggle during those occasions when the South African force in the south of Angola near Dicinkulene area most of the Soviet equipment captured as it was not part of their doctrine was offered to UNITA. Anti-aircraft guns, long reach guns, all this equipment, throughout the peacetime was being rehabilitated by UNITA. If you add this to the material being imported, merely increased the potential or the mechanised assets for the force that UNITA was organising. In other words, with what UNITA bought, with what it had hidden, and with what it rehabilitated, the number was big.

UNITA also had three regional hospitals at Mavinga, Jamba and Mucusso but seriously injured soldiers were sent to a military hospital in Pretoria where there was a ward exclusively for UNITA patients. As part of his overall strategy of controlling his commanders, Savimbi placed UNITA leadership families unobserved and under his direct control in a remote south-eastern corner of Angola called Boa Esperanza. This was where UNITA had schools for the children of the leadership as well as old age homes and orphanages.

Retired SADF Senior UNITA Liaison officer Colonel Fred Oelschig also had this to say about UNITA:

UNITA would regularly rout FAPLA forces from their headquarters at Jamba in south east Angola, well outside the operational ability of the MPLA government. UNITA was able to expand their area of direct influence to include Kwando Cubango province by 1985. This area they proclaimed as Free Angola where their supporters had freedom of movement with absolutely no military threat from FAPLA. Within this area, they had schools, clinics, industries and farms. There was a postal service, a trade union, airports, a student bursary system and sent their brightest students to University in Portugal and elections. The UNITA legal system catered for every form of criminal offence from stealing, poaching to murder. They had orphanages, old age homes, ten different church denominations represented by missionaries and pastors and they had three large, well-equipped regional hospitals. UNITA also had a well-structured militia in the rural areas armed with weapons dating back to the Portuguese era and radio communication.

Savimbi divided UNITA into five fronts commanded by a general or brigadier rank, each of which was then sub-divided into 22 regions under colonel rank and then further divided into sectors and zones under lesser rank.

UNITA also had special forces or penetration groups, small, highly specialised and well-trained groups whose main function was to infiltrate deep into FAPLA rear areas. They were tasked with disrupting FAPLA logistical routes especially storage and strategic facilities as well as deep reconnaissance, ambushes and mine laying. In addition there were the BATE groups that specialised in sabotage actions and were well trained in the use of explosives. These groups carried out sabotage actions against strategic targets such as oil-producing facilities and other infrastructure.

An undoubted genius at organisation as well as command and control, Savimbi had several talented commanders who escaped suspicion and execution to conduct an extended guerrilla war for nearly three decades. It was as if Savimbi was prescient enough to leave his best men untouched by the regular bloodletting for which he became notorious. These men who managed to survive the war included Chief of Staff Demosthenes Amos Chilingutila, Brigadier Geraldo Sachipengo Nunda the Northern Front Commander

General Ben Ben, Cangonga railway station, 1983. (Piet Nortje)

General Arlindo Pena in FAPLA uniform. (Demarte Dachala Pena)

in 1984 and later chief of the Angolan Armed Forces, General Eugenio Manuvakola who defected to government forces in 1997, General Abel Chivukuvuku who was arrested in 1992 after the failed election and General Samuel Chiwale. Premier among them was Savimbi's nephew, Arlindo Chenda Isaac Pena, more popularly known as General Ben Ben.

A 1984 assessment by United States Marine Corps Robert R. Major illustrates the talents of General Ben Ben as a military commander.

> In February 1983, UNITA captured Cangonga on the Benguela Railroad. The manner in which it was taken not only shows the detail in planning made but also the sophistication of the force involved. Battalion 017, commanded by Colonel Ben-Ben Arlindo Pena, 28 years of age, had constructed a relief model the size of a badminton court of the town and its approaches to use for the battle briefing. Colored roads, arches, bark, twigs, and moss were used in the model town to symbolize the buildings and fortifications of Cangonga. Battalion 017 conducted endless rehearsals. The battalion consisted of 520 regular troops armed with 75mm cannons, 81mm mortars, RPG-7 antitank missiles, AK-47 rifles, a 45-strong platoon of 'Special Forces,' a 50-strong logistics team, 25 demolitions specialists, some 300 guerrillas, and a long chain

of young men and women carrying ammunition on their heads. Finally, at 0300 on 11 February, a single rifle shot signaled that all units of Battalion 017 were in position. At 0500 the attack began. The MPLA's arsenal exploded and the entire town was soon ablaze. The MPLA garrison was stunned! Most of the 300 defenders fled. UNITA killed or captured the remainder. The importance of Cangonga's capture was two-fold. First, it allowed a secure supply line to be pushed to regular forces and guerrillas who had already infiltrated 200 miles north of the Benguela Railroad. This would help UNITA fulfil one of its major objectives of creating a corridor of 'liberated' territory right up the centre of the country to where a salient of Zaire juts into north central Angola. This would cut off the territory held by the MPLA in the east from its areas in the west. The significance of Cangonga's capture, however, lay in its propaganda value. UNITA wanted to show Western journalists as well as its own people that its forces were highly skilled and motivated, and fully capable of striking the MPLA in the very heart of Angola with a surgical precision devoid of help from external sources, especially South Africa.

In a relationship not unlike Stalin and his consistently successful military commander, Marshal Zhukov, Savimbi managed to hold on to some of his better commanders for a period before losing most to paranoia, defection, surrender or capture. This was a scenario that played out for other guerrilla leaders of the past including Simon Bolivar and Mao Zedong.

The most lethal UNITA defection was Brigadier Geraldo Sachipengo Nunda who ultimately joined the government team that led to the killing of Jonas Savimbi in 2002.

By 2002 Savimbi had avoided several peace initiatives and an election but he had also lost much territory and military assets to the point of being hunted by a dedicated team from many backgrounds and nationalities. Africa's most enduring bush fighter was 67 years old when he was killed by hubris, not bullets.

CHAPTER 10

VELUPILLAI PRABHAKARAN, SRI LANKA

The most audacious start of the career of any guerrilla leader was the 1975 up-close-and-personal assassination of the mayor of Jaffna in the former British colony of Ceylon, now Sri Lanka, by 18-year-old Velupillai Prabhakaran, the future leader of the insurgent group, the Tamil Tigers.

Ceylon had a long and rich history before British occupation, there was a Sinhalese majority population and a Tamil minority centred in the north close to the Indian sea border with which the Tamil had ancestral ties. The Indian state of Tamil Nadu is a mere 22 miles away from Jaffna across the Palk Strait.

Independence as a republic came to the new Sri Lanka in 1972, but the Tamils, both local and Indian, experienced discrimination in citizenship, education and development. Agitation for an autonomous Tamil state called Tamil Eelam began in earnest from the 1960s culminating in the creation of a Tamil military force called the Liberation Tigers of Tamil Eelam or LTTE by Velupillai Prabhakaran in 1976 with the sole objective of establishing an independent Tamil state.

The world has had a long history of ethnic-based conflict, the most recent being the Rohingya cleansing in Myanmar, with many guerrilla movements emanating from ethnicity such as the native uprising against Spanish rulers in South America led by Simon Bolivar or the insurgency of the American Revolution against

One of the weapons in the guerrilla arsenal is **simple provocation**. Whether a symbolic peaceful protest that descends into violence or an orchestrated atrocity, both are designed to provoke an excessive reaction by authorities that leads to reactionary recruitment and sympathy for the cause. Past provocations include the Declaration of Death against the Spanish by Simon Bolivar, protest newspapers and demonstrations organised by Mao Zedong and the famous self-immolation of a Buddhist monk during the Vietnam War.

the British. What is certain is that if a nationalist movement fails to succeed, it will continue to fester until basic goals are met for autonomy and equality. This is not restricted to third-world rural populations but the developed regions of Europe such as the Catalan independence movement in Spain.

Prabhakaran trod the well-worn path of guerrilla leadership that concentrated on building a multi-faceted military force, obtain financing by any means necessary and the holy grail – international recognition. Like the FARC of Colombia, he was destined to only achieve the first two, unlike the FARC, he chose disintegration before integration. The LTTE leader was a gifted organiser but a fatalist visionary who saw the creation of territory under LTTE control with civil administration, media outlets, the elements of a local economy and a LTTE that had land, air and sea branches unlike most guerrilla movements. It was in fact, a shadow government.

The LTTE took some time to develop into a sufficiently cogent force before undertaking their first major attack in July 1983, at night near the provincial capital of Jaffna, which started with a road ambush using a bomb, that led to the deaths of 15 government soldiers including an officer. It was a basic of guerrilla warfare; a surprise overwhelming attack on familiar territory leading to an early victory for an insurgent force seeking notoriety to enable recruitment. The longer game was the inevitable reprisal of Singhalese natives against the Tamils

Velupillai Prabhakaran. (Tamilnet/ Wikimedia Commons)

leading to Black July, the destruction of shops and businesses as well as the murder of thousands of Tamils, many of whom fled the country permanently.

The Sinhalese-driven pogrom crystallised donations and sent Tamil youth into the open arms of the LTTE who began to rise from obscurity to a national prominence that eventually led to open civil war and a government besieged for nearly three decades. Jonas Savimbi had a Sri Lankan doppelganger who failed to absorb the lessons of the past, so was consigned to repeat it with deadly effect.

Somewhat akin to the relationship between Pakistan's intelligence service and the Taliban, the LTTE had received logistical and training support from the Indian intelligence service known as RAW or the Research and Analysis Wing at various periods during the civil war. As part of this operation Prabhakaran and several LTTE commanders received small arms training in an isolated forest reserve of south-east India called Sirumalai, but there was an ongoing presence in India of LTTE operatives to facilitate financial and logistical support for the insurgency.

LTTE training in India was only part of a strict regime promoted for the cadre by Prabhakaran that included abstinence and a cyanide necklace that Tamil Tigers showed no reluctance in using when pushed into a corner or captured. 1984 saw a massive increase in LTTE attacks that included the landmine killing of

A stripped Tamil youth at a bus stop, July 1983. (Chandragupta Amarasinghe/Wikimedia)

the Sri Lanka Army (SLA) Northern commander as well as an attack on the Chavakachcheri police station, east of Jaffna, which was completely destroyed and 24 policemen killed, both taking place in November. The following January the LTTE blew up the highly secure Jaffna–Colombo train, killing 28 Sri Lankan Army soldiers. The next significant LTTE operation took place in the rebel heartland of Mullitivu district at the town of Kokkilai on the north-east coast of Sri Lanka in February 1985. The target was a government army barracks that suffered 13 losses before the attack was repulsed. In April 1985 the Jaffna police station was attacked and damaged while the Mannar police station on a peninsula south of Jaffna was destroyed in May with five policemen killed and four taken prisoner. LTTE attacks, like all guerrilla campaigns, were not limited to legitimate military targets. The following May, when a group of LTTE rebels drove

LTTE Court Kilinochchi district, 2005. (Mugilan/Wikimedia)

a commandeered vehicle into Anuradhapura, south of Mannar, they killed over 100 innocent civilians.

The civil war took a proximate turn in May 1986 when the LTTE blew up Air Lanka flight 512 at the Bandaranaike International Airport, a few miles north of the capital city, Colombo. The Tristar aircraft was completely destroyed with 21 of the 128 passengers killed and dozens injured, many of whom were foreigners. By 1986 the LTTE had occupied Jaffna and parts of the peninsula. The government of Sri Lanka appeared to be under siege, not unlike the government of Colombia when FARC attacks essentially confined security to major urban centres in 1998.

In May 1987 the government of Sri Lanka decided to reverse exclusive LTTE occupation with Operation *Vadamarachchi* or *Liberation* that ultimately became a siege endeavour by the Sri Lankan forces, leading to hundreds of casualties on both sides with no clear result. It seemed too much of a coincidence that two SLA commanders of this operation were later killed by a landmine in 1992 on Kayts Island east of Jaffna. By June the SLA had reached the outskirts of Jaffna only to have the Indian government intervene with an airdrop of relief supplies for the residents of Jaffna.

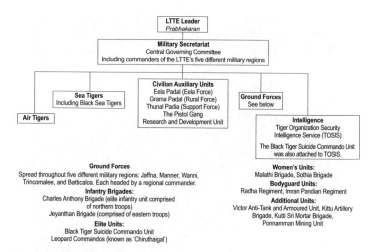

LTTE military wing, 2002. (The Centre on Conflict, Development and Peace Building)

This precipitated the low point of the Indian LTTE connection with the two governments signing the Indo-Sri Lankan accord which facilitated an Indian Peace Keeping Force (IPKF) to enter northern Sri Lanka to disarm the LTTE. The LTTE immediately began attacks on the IPKF during their three-year tenure until political pressure from within Sri Lanka and India forced the Indian withdrawal in March 1990. During that period the IPKF had several battles with the LTTE in an effort to clear the LTTE from the Jaffna Peninsula, but in the end the LTTE ceded the territory in true guerrilla fashion and sought sanctuary in the surrounding population and jungle. The LTTE had one outstanding success in October 1987 during the IPKF occupation when an attempted Indian commando raid to capture the LTTE leadership at Jaffna University was ambushed leading to 33 Indian soldiers being killed. This was a reverse Washington at Trenton where local intelligence on a foreign army in unfamiliar territory led to an insurgent victory, a scenario replayed throughout the centuries.

The last Indian casualty of the IPKF intervention was Prime Minister Rajiv Gandhi who was killed by a female LTTE suicide bomber in May 1991.

LTTE Sea Tiger boat, 2003. (Ulflarsen/Wikimedia)

In June 1990 the LTTE took advantage of the IPKF withdrawal to launch a siege attack on a Sri Lankan Army base at Kokavil in Mullaitivu district where the beginning of the end for the LTTE took place nearly two decades later. LTTE forces had prevented SLA reinforcement or substantial re-supply leading to the decimation of nearly 50 SLA soldiers and capture of the garrison. There was more of this to come in the following years by a well-organised and supplied LTTE organisation led by Prabhakaran who ultimately chose military success over wise expenditure of political capital.

A modern exception to the UNITA or LTTE model of military overuse over political compromise can be found in Afghanistan or the Houthi insurgency in Yemen, both of which have displayed the signs of an endless rebellion that may require peace on their terms or a buffer zone.

Between 1990 and 1995 there was a see-saw between the LTTE and the SLA as they fought to control territory most of it in favor of the government side including a sustained attack on the choke point Elephant Pass army base in July 1991 that included modified heavy equipment which has seen much prominence recently in the Syrian civil war. Although the attack was repulsed over a sustained period that required large SLA reinforcement, hundreds died on both sides. Reminiscent of Khe Sanh during the Vietnam War, the self-same base was later captured by the LTTE in 2000 only to be finally re-captured in 2009.

Captured LTTE armoured bulldozer from Battle of Elephant Pass, 1991. (AntanO/Wikipedia)

The LTTE is widely believed to have been responsible for the assassination of the President of Sri Lanka by a bicycle-borne IED during this period in May 1993. Prabhakaran developed and implemented a Tamil Tiger division called the Black Tigers whose mandate was explosive suicide missions on all manner of targets. Much of this knowledge is believed to have come from Palestinian sources of the LTTE who were not shy, as with all guerrillas, in seeking out friends in any available place.

Unlike many guerrilla armies whose tenures have consisted of isolated skirmishes and the temporary occupation of urban areas, the LTTE had several massive battles with the SLA as it sought a single knock-out punch to occupy the entire Jaffna peninsula. Although successful on many occasions in taking a military objective, the LTTE were unable to translate these into overall victories or the creation of an independent Tamil state. Prabhakaran was unafraid of committing large resources in these efforts which produced daring successes at the cost of depleting his military might.

In November 1993 the LTTE overran a Sri Lankan naval base at Pooneryn, south of Jaffna, and captured tanks and ammunition

LTTE bicycle platoon, 2004. (Wikimedia)

while destroying some government boats at a cost of nearly a thousand casualties on each side.

Like Simon Bolivar, Mao Zedong and Jonas Savimbi, Prabhakaran kept a close watch on his leadership. Close friend and fellow commander, Gopalaswamy Mahendraraja or Mahattaya had been second in command of the LTTE before being relieved of command in 1992, arrested in 1993 and then executed in December 1994, allegedly for plotting against Prabhakaran and/or being an agent of the Indian intelligence unit, RAW.

The leader of an extended guerrilla campaign will often use a peace treaty or ceasefire to relieve any unbearable military pressure or provide a needed hiatus for enhanced logistics and recruitment. Such was the case of the Colombian government demilitarised zone gift to the FARC in 1998 and the LTTE ceasefire with the government in January 1995 which allowed the LTTE to retain territory, control and their arms. By the following April the LTTE blasted this arrangement by sinking two SRI Lanka Navy ships and killing 22 sailors.

Between 1995 and 2001 there was another series of battles also known as Eealam III, starting with the siege of Jaffna in October 1995 which saw hundreds of casualties on both sides and the LTTE fleeing from the fixed positions that have never worked for an insurgency. Yet again, the LTTE, like the Red Army of China, the Viet Cong of Vietnam, UNITA of Angola and the FARC of

Colombia, simply retreated into the safety of the surrounding jungle. Despite government pronouncements that the LTTE were finished, the following December rebels attacked an SLA unit on a narrow strip of the eastern coastline halfway down the length of Sri Lanka at Batticaloa, a classic guerrilla choke point ambush that left 33 soldiers and one officer dead.

This was followed up in July 1996 with a significant LTTE victory that saw a large, isolated Sri Lankan army base at Mullativu along a narrow coast strip almost surrounded by water, demolished with over 1,000 dead government soldiers, a navy ship sunk, artillery seized and a large area ceded to the insurgents.

In all this, Prabhakaran was a military genius but not a political one. Attacks almost certainly involved the collection of intelligence over an extended period of time on government forces at a fixed position – surveillance that could have been undertaken by any local. There would have been numerous reviews and rehearsals as the guerrillas employed their most valuable asset, time, which afforded a strike at the optimum opportunity and convenience of the attackers, a scenario repeated throughout the Sri Lankan civil war. Another facet of the LTTE was the mass execution of captured government soldiers which was certain to have a demoralising effect up to a point, but the tables can be turned when government troops commit similar atrocities, as shown in the final battle for the LTTE in 2009 where SLA units proved they were capable of equal ferocity. Battlefield executions are not confined to Sri Lanka but have occurred throughout insurgencies worldwide including the destruction of the French Groupement Mobile No.100 at Mang Yang Pass in Vietnam after Dien Bien Phu in 1954.

The LTTE and SLA conducted a series of attacks against each other over the next few years, neither being able to score a complete victory. In July 2001 the LTTE conducted their best operation with a second raid on the Bandaranaike International Airport and the nearby Katunayake military airbase with fewer than a dozen men carrying small arms several hundred miles from their home base. The attack on the air force base destroyed many bombers, helicopters and even transport aircraft while the civilian airport had three Airbus passenger aircraft destroyed at a high cost – no small blow to the economy of Sri Lanka during a time of war. The many passengers waiting to board were lucky not to have been killed or kidnapped.

Sitting in his jungle bunker, Prabhakaran must have felt smug. But this feeling was not to last long. By December LTTE had begun negotiations through Norwegian intermediaries with President Chandrika Kumaratunga who had lost an eye to a LTTE attack in 2001 that killed dozens. The LTTE seemingly dropped a demand for independence and after a written agreement and mutual ceasefire, Norwegian monitors entered the country to try to finalise and maintain the peace treaty. The politics of the day and the recent airport attack had created an atmosphere of great desire for peace which the LTTE capitalised on before abandoning negotiations in 2003.

After the peace treaty ended, the Jaffna Peninsula was isolated from the rest of Sri Lanka by the LTTE except by sea and the Tamil Tigers attacked the government naval base at Trincomalee on the eastern coast in 2006 as well as defensive positions leading to Jaffna. These attacks were repulsed and a later attack by the SLA from Jaffna failed, although it caused nearly a thousand government casualties. What followed was a pattern of attacks by both sides that characterised the pre-treaty period, resumed in futility. The last LTTE notable success was a 2007 joint attack by their air force and Black Tiger suicide soldiers on the government Anuradhapura Air Force Base in central Sri Lanka, a great distance from their home territory, which resulted in the loss of ten aircraft, mostly helicopters.

Of the many novel features of the LTTE multi-decade insurgency, which include entire suicide units consisting of women and widespread IED usage by LTTE personnel, bicycle and vehicle, a small air force must have been the zenith of guerrilla aspiration at the time, eclipsed more recently by ISIS IED drone attacks in Iraq and Syria.

The end for the LTTE and Velupillai Prabhakaran drew near in December 2005 with the appointment of General Sarath Fonseka to head the Sri Lankan Army. Fonseka had extensive training both locally and internationally before entering the fray in 1987 to participate in several operations. He distinguished himself not

General Sarath Fonseka, 2009. (Rajith Vidanaarachchi/ Wikimedia)

only by surviving the early part of the conflict while fighting an enemy known to target commanders but in 1991 at the first battle of Elephant Pass when he led the 3rd Brigade as part of a sea-borne siege relief operation that endured for several weeks.

Colonel Fonseka gained further attention when he led the Midnight Express operation in 1993 that saved hundreds of trapped SLA troops in the Jaffna Fort. Later that year during the Yal Devi operation to destroy LTTE lagoon facilities at Kilali, the SLA was ambushed and Fonseka was struck by shrapnel. He was among hundreds wounded and killed. He then held a series of posts before 2000 when he was urgently drafted in as a commander to help resist LTTE attempts to re-take Jaffna after they captured the Elephant Pass camp. By 2005 Lieutenant-General Fonseka had been promoted several times and was based at Army Headquarters in Colombo, where he was severely injured by an LTTE female suicide bomber in 2006. It was the first such incident in several years in the capital and it focused on Fonseka as a high-value target.

The attacker wore explosives arranged to give an impression of pregnancy and pretended to attend a nearby maternity clinic before detonating herself as the famed commander approached.

On his return to the fray, Fonseka pursued a strategy that included more coordinated attacks between army, navy and air force as well as targeted assassinations and intelligence gathering by small long-range reconnaissance teams who could call on helicopters for exfiltration.

What followed was a series of LTTE defeats at the hands of the SLA that included the capture of Vidattaltivu on the north-east coast in July 2008 – an area which had been under LTTE control for decades; the LTTE capital of Kilinochchi in December 2008; the LTTE stronghold of Mullaitivu in January 2009; and the final re-capture of the Elephant Pass camp, also in January. It was more reminiscent of a German *blitzkrieg* during World War II than a tropical guerrilla war, with heavy reliance on air and artillery power to clear the way for soldiers in the field. Proper resources, training and adapted modern tactics without political interference played a major role in these advances.

The last LTTE stronghold, Puthukkudiyirippu, was taken the following April and the few remaining LTTE soldiers and leaders were isolated on a spit of land where they were gradually obliterated including Velupillai Prabhakaran, who was killed on the morning of 19 May 2009.

Fonseka, the military hero of Sri Lanka, almost came to the same fate as Cuban General Arnaldo Ochoa who was executed by the Cuban Caudillo upon his return from Angola. He was imprisoned in 2010 and released in 2012, further evidence of the well-known truth that a military leader should be careful not to be more popular than his political chief.

SOURCES

GENERAL/INTRODUCTION

Appiah, Kwame Anthony and Gates, Jr., Henry Louis. *Africana: The Encyclopedia of the African and African American Experience*. London, Oxford University Press, 2005.

Freeman, Michael. *Financing Terrorism: Case Studies*. Routledge, 2016.

Giles, Lionel (trans). *Sun Tzu on the Art of War: The Oldest Military Treatise in the World*. British Museum, 1910.

James Joes, Anthony. *Modern Guerrilla Insurgency*, Praeger Publishers, 1992, 109

Loveman, Brian & Davies, Jr., Thomas M. *Che Guevara Guerrilla Warfare*, University of Nebraska Press, 1985.

Norton-Taylor, Richard. 'Asymmetric Warfare', *The Guardian* (3 October 2001).

O'Kane, Rosemary H. T. *Terrorism*. Routledge, 2013.

O'Leary (Ret.), Colonel Jeff. *The Centurion Principles: Battlefield Lessons for Frontline Leaders*. Thomas Nelson, 1982.

Rothstein, Hy & Whaley, Barton. *The Art and Science of Military Deception*. Artech House, 2013.

Whittaker, David J. *The Terrorism Reader Second Edition*. Routledge, 2001.

1. WILLIAM WALLACE, SCOTLAND

Barrow, G. W. S. *Robert Bruce and the community of the realm of Scotland*, Universiy of California Press, 1965.

Brown, Chris. *William Wallace: the true story of Braveheart*. Tempus Publishing, 2005.

Grant, George. *The Life and Adventures of Sir William Wallace: Liberator of Scotland*. J. Menzies, 1851.

King, Andy & Simpkin, David. *England and Scotland at War. c.1296–c.1513*. Brill, 2012.

Murison, A. F. *William Wallace Guardian of Scotland*. Dover Publications, 2003.

Murison, A. F. *Sir William Wallace*, Edinburgh: Oliphant. Anderson and Ferrier, 1898.

Prestwich, Michael, *The Wallace Book*, John Donald, 2007.

Watson, Reverend J. S. *Sir William Wallace, The Scottish Hero: A narrative of his Life and Actions.* Saunders, Otley and Company, 1861.

2. GENERAL GEORGE WASHINGTON, AMERICA

Burg, David F. *The American Revolution.* Facts on File, 2007.

Fischer, David Hackett. *Washington's Crossing.* Oxford University Press, 2004.

Grizzard Jr., Frank E. *George! A Guide to All Things Washington.* Mariner Publishing, 2005.

Kennedy, Francis H. *The American Revolution: A Historical Guidebook.* Oxford University Press, 2014.

Lanning, Michael Lee. *The American Revolution 100.* Sourcebooks, 2008.

Lillback, Peter A. with Newcombe, Jerry. *George Washington's Sacred Fire.* Providence Forum Press, 2006.

Peacock, Judith. *The Battles of Lexington and Concord.* Bridgestone Books, 2002.

Tucker, Phillip Thomas. *George Washington's Surprise Attack.* Skyhorse Publishing, 2014.

Wells, J. W. *An Alphabetical List of the Battles of the War of the Rebellion with Dates.* N.A. Strait, 1875.

3. SIMON BOLIVAR, VENEZUELA

Arana, Marie. Bolivar: *American Liberator.* New York. Simon and Schuster, 2013.

Brown, Matthew. *Adventuring Through Spanish Colonies: Simón Bolívar, Foreign Mercenaries and the Birth of New Nations.* Liverpool University Press, 2006.

Clayton, Lawrence A. & Conniff, Michael L. *A History of Modern Latin America.* Wadsworth, 2005.

Lynch, John. *Simon Bolivar A Life.* Yale University Press, 2006.

Reis, Ronald A. *Simon Bolivar.* Chelsea House, 2013.

Slatta, Richard W. & De Grummond, Jane Lucas. *Simon Bolivar's Quest for Glory.* Texas A & M University Press, 2003.

4. KOOS DE LA REY, SOUTH AFRICA

Badsey, Stephen. *Doctrine and Reform in the British Cavalry 1880–1918.* Ashgate Publishing, 2008.

Miller. Stephen M. *Lord Methuen and the British Army: Failure and Redemption in South Africa.* Frank Cass, 1999.

Olson, James S. and Shadle, Robert. *Historical Dictionary of the British Empire.* Greenwood Press, 1996.

South African History Online, *Jacobus Hercules de la Rey*
www.britishbattles.com, Battle of Modder River

5. KING ABDUL AZIZ BIN ABDUL RAHMAN AL SAUD, SAUDI ARABIA

Al-Nafjan, Dr. Fahad M. *The Origins of Saudi-American Relations.* Arab Scientific Publishers, 2010.

Bowen, Wayne H. *The History of Saudi Arabia.* Greenwood Press, 2008.

Simons, Geoff. *Saudi Arabia: The Shape of a Client Feudalism.* Macmillan Press, 1998.

Tucker, Spencer C. *The Encyclopedia of the Arab-Israeli Conflict.* ABC-CLIO, 2008.

Winegard, Timothy C. *The First World Oil War.* University of Toronto Press, 2016.

Wynbrandt, James. *A Brief History of Saudi Arabia.* Facts on File, 2004.

Zuhur, Sherifa. *Saudi Arabia.* ABC-CLIO, 2011.

6. MAO ZEDONG, CHINA

Chang, Jung & Halliday, Jon. *Mao: The Unknown Story.* Anchor Books, 2005.

Fairbank, John King and Goldman, Merle. *China a New History.* Harvard University Press, 1992.

Feigon, Lee. *Mao: A Reinterpretation.* Ivan R. Dee, 2002.

Gay, Kathlyn. *Mao Zedong's China.* Twenty First Century Books, 2008.

Graff, David Andrew and Higham, Robin. *A Military History of China.* The University Press of Kentucky, 2012.

Gruhl, Werner. *Imperial Japan's World War Two: 1931–1945.* Transaction Publishers, 2007.

Li, Xiaobing. *China at War: An Encyclopedia.* ABC-CLIO, 2012.

Pantsov, Alexander V. *Mao: The Real Story,* Simon and Schuster, 2007.

Siao-Yu. *Mao Tse-Tung and I Were Beggars.* Syracuse University Press, 1959.

Slavicek, Louise Chipley. *Mao Zedong.* Chelsea House Publishers, 2004.

Tanner, Harold M. *China a History.* Hackett Publishing, 2009.

Wales, Nym. *Red Dust.* Stanford University Press, 1952.

Wortzel, Larry M. *Dictionary of Contemporary Chinese Military History.* Greenwood Press, 1999.

Zedong, Mao. *Quotations from Chairman Mao* Zedong (The Little Red Book). 1946.

7. GENERAL VO NGUYEN GIAP, VIETNAM

Currey, Cecil B. *Victory at any cost. The genius of Viet Nam's Gen. Vo Nguyen Giap.* Potomac Books, 1997.

Fall, Bernard. *Street Without Joy: The French Debacle in Indochina*. Stackpole Military History, 1961.

Greer, Bob. *Journey Among Heroes*. Trafford Publishing, 2011.

Langguth, A. J. *Our Vietnam The War 1954–1975*. Simon and Shuster, 2000.

Tucker, Spencer C. *The Encyclopedia of the Vietnam War*. ABC-CLIO, 2011.

Waite, James. *The End of the First Indochina War: A Global History*. Routledge, 2012.

Wiest, Andrew A. *The Vietnam War*. Rosen Publishing Group, 2009.

Willbanks, James H. *Vietnam War: The Essential Reference Guide*. ABC-CLIO, 2013.

Zhai, Qiang. *China and the Vietnam Wars 1950–1975*. The University of North Carolina Press, 2000.

8. MANUEL MARULANDA, COLOMBIA

Calvert, Peter. *A Political and Economic Dictionary of Latin America*. Europa Publications, 2004.

Henderson, James D. *Colombia's Narcotics Nightmare: How the Drug Trade Destroyed Peace*. McFarland and Company, 2015.

Kline, Harvey F. Historical Dictionary of Colombia. The Scarecrow Press, 2012.

Mendez, Juan E. *Political Murder and Reform in Colombia*. Human Rights Watch, 1992.

Rabasa, Angel and Chalk, Peter. *Colombian Labrynth*. Rand, 2001.

Rinehart, Christine Sixta. *Volatile Social Movements and the Origins of Terrorism*. Lexington Books, 2013.

Ruiz, Bert. *The Colombian Civil War*. McFarland and Company, 2001.

Shifter, Michael. *Plan Colombia: A Retrospective. Americas Quarterly*, Summer 2012.

Wylie, Leslie. *Colombia's Forgotten Frontier: A Literary Geography of the Putumayo*. Liverpool University Press, 2013.

9. JONAS SAVIMBI, ANGOLA

Angola Constitution and Citizenship Laws Handbook: Strategic Information and Basic Laws. Washington, International Business Publications, Washington, 2014.

Burke, Major Robert R. USMC, *UNITA – A Case Study in Modern Insurgency*. Marine Corps Command and Staff College, 2 April 1984.

George, Edward. *The Cuban Intervention in Angola. 1965–1991: From Che Guevara to Cuito Cuanavale*. Frank Cass, 2005.

Guimaraes, Fernando Andresen. *The Origins of the Angolan Civil War: Foreign Intervention and Domestic Political Conflict*. London, Palgrave MacMillan, 2001.

James III, W. Martin. *A Political History of the Civil War in Angola: 1974–1990*.

Transaction Publishers, New Brunswick and London, 1992.

Kikkuk, Leon. *Letters to Gabriela: Angola's Last War for Peace. What the UN Did and Why*. Florida Literary Foundation, 2005.

Polack, Peter. *Last Hot Battle of the Cold War*. Casemate, 2013.

Vakunta, Peter Wuteh. *A Nation at Risk: A Personal Narrative of the Cameroonian Crisis*. Bloomington, IUniverse Inc, 2012.

Wright, George. *The Destruction of a Nation: United States' Policy Towards Angola Since 1945*. London, Pluto Press,1997.

10. VELUPILLAI PRABHAKARAN, SRI LANKA

Bandarage, Asoka. *The Separatist Conflict in Sri Lanka: Terrorism, ethnicity, political economy*, Routledge, 2009.

Brown, Derek. *The deadly tigers of Sri Lanka. The Guardian*, 24 July 2001.

Dissanayaka, T. D. S. A. *The Dilemma of Sri Lanka: An In-depth Account of the Current Ethnic Conflict in Sri Lanka*, Swastika (Pvt.) Limited, 1993.

Goodhand, Jonathan, Korf, Benedikt and Spencer, Jonathan. *Conflict and Peacebuilding in Sri Lanka: Caught in the Peace Trap?* Routledge, 2011.

Hashim, Ahmed. *When Counterinsurgency Wins: Sri Lanka's Defeat of the Tamil Tigers*. University of Pennsylvania Press, 2013.Rajah, A. R. Munasinghe, Sarath, Major General. *A Soldier's Version: An account of the on-going conflict and the origin of terrorism in Sri Lanka*. MIS, 2000.

Sriskanda. *Government and Politics in Sri Lanka: Biopolitics and Security*, Routledge, 2017.

Richards, Joanne. *An Institutional History of the Liberation Tigers of Tamil Eelam*, The Centre on Conflict, Development and Peacebuilding, November 2014.

Rinehart, Christine Sixta. *Volatile Social Movements and the Origins of Terrorism: The Radicalization of Change*. Lexington Books, 2013.

Wickremesekera, Channa. *The Tamil Separatist War in Sri Lanka*. Routledge, 2016.

ACKNOWLEDGEMENTS

To my devoted family who feed the beast and remind everyone the fence is to keep him in, not to keep you out.

To the real-life guerrilla kings, Commandantes Camilo, Bravo and Francisco.

Mention must be made of a great influence on many young Latin Americans by Commandante Cero, Eden Pastora, whom I had the honour to briefly meet near Nicoya, Costa Rica in Christmas 1991. He has survived many assassinations of his person and character but nevertheless influenced generations in the purity of *la lucha*. His greatest endeavour was to successfully kidnap the Nicaraguan Congress in 1978 to ensure the release of his comrades. When he was only eight, members of the Somoza security apparatus killed his father. From acorns do oak trees grow.

Mi Companero desde La Tierra Pura Vida, Miguel Ortega, who introduced me to Commandante Cero.

Mohammed Baldi for production of the King Ibn Saud You Tube video.

Ruth Sheppard, Isobel Nettleton, Connor Reason, Carlie Rivera and the entire Casemate team for great persistence, hard work and talent.

Jill Louise Replogle for assistance and kindness with the iconic Commandante Cero (Eden Pastora) photo from The Tico Times of Costa Rica.

Peter Harrington of the Anne S. K. Brown Military Collection, Brown University Library for generous permission to use the George Washington images.

Jo Woolf for the picture of Cambuskenneth Abbey.

Andy Hillhouse and the William Wallace Society for the depiction of the William Wallace Trial in London.

Wikimedia Commons source without which many images would be unavailable.

Thanks to the Etna Labuschagne of the Anglo-Boer War Museum of Bloemfontein for use of material on General Koos de la Rey.

To my staunch supporters at The Edge restaurant headed by the world citizen, Philippe Gros.

Shane Aquart aka Dreddy for proofing some chapters.

Maggie Giglioli for kindly reading and adding to my manuscript.

Saudi Arabia diplomat Naif Alhantushi for helpful input on King Ibn Saud.

Outstanding You Tube producer Arrian Yates for assistance with book videos for You Tube.

Pamela McDonough-Brown for perfect Scot accent narration on William Wallace video.

Clare Litt of Casemate who championed publication of this effort.

To my devoted nephews and guerrilla leaders Nick, Justin, Cole, Wesley and Tanner who tire me out with a barrage of compliments that I am the best Uncle.

INDEX